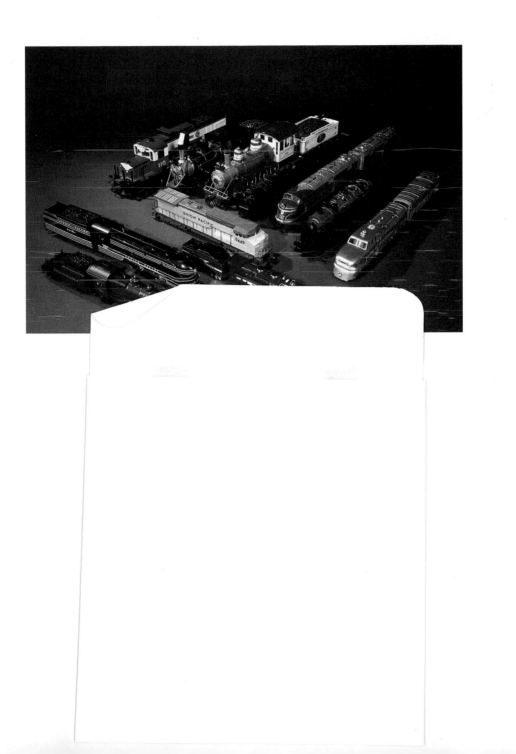

Modern Toy Trains

GERRY AND JANET SOUTER

MBI Publishing Company

Dedication

This book is dedicated to the hard-working representatives of the toy train manufacturers featured in this book. Their efforts and goodwill made it possible: Kelly Rice, Weaver Models; Kristin Bailey, MTH-RailKing; Larry Harrington, Williams Electric Trains; Rob Sementek, Bachmann Trains; David Buffington, LGB; Jeff Cohen, MDK K-Line; Kate Hannett, Atlas O; and Sandi Flynn, Marx Trains.

First published in 2002 by MBI Publishing Company, Galtier Plaza, 380 Jackson Street, Suite 200, St. Paul, MN 55101-3885 USA

© Gerry and Janet Souter, 2002

MBI Publishing Company books are also available at discounts in bulk quantity for industrial or sales-promotional use. For details write to Special Sales Manager at Motorbooks International Wholesalers & Distributors, Galtier Plaza, 380 Jackson Street, Suite 200, St. Paul, MN 55101-3885 USA.

Library of Congress Cataloging-in-Publication Data Available
ISBN 1-7603-1179-X

Edited by Dennis Pernu
Designed by LeAnn Kuhlmann

Printed in China

On the front cover: This Union Pacific Challenger rolled out of the Williams shop in 1989, an all-brass 30-inch scale model with nickel drivers, two smoke units, and electronic reverse. These offshore-built, limited-run jewels set the trend that all manufacturers would follow in 12 years. *Courtesy Williams Electric Trains*

On the frontispiece: This collection of modern toy trains features most of the primary manufacturers from the last 30 years. Back row, left to right: LGB White Pass diesel and LGB Mogul 2-6-0 steam locomotive, both in G scale; Bachmann Ringmaster 4-6-0 in Large Scale *Elaine Silets Collection;* Lionel 6200 Pennsylvania Railroad steam turbine and Rock Island E6 A-A diesel *Mike Moore Collection;* MTH 2-8-8-2 Triplex Erie steam locomotive and MTH O gauge Aerotrain *MTH-RailKing;* Front row, front to back: K-Line B-6sb switcher in Pennsy colors *MDK K-Line;* Weaver brass Lehigh Valley shrouded 4-6-2 JohnWilkes steamer (Weaver Models); Marx Trains' 0-4-0 Marlines steamer *Marx Trains;* Williams Union Pacific Dash 8 *Williams Electric Trains*

On the title page: The original K-Line GP38 had matured considerably by 1999. Offered in a number of paint jobs, the model also found its voice with K-Line's own "Real Sounds." *Courtesy MDK K-Line*

On the back cover: Top: SD40 diesels were the big haulers of their day, and are still used in lash-ups today. Lionel's 1983 No. 8376 was part of the 1361 Gold Coast Edition set. *Courtesy Carail Museum, Detroit, Michigan; Bottom:* Without a doubt one of the gaudiest paint jobs ever slapped on the venerable Hudson 4-6-4, this 2001 O gauge creation is based on a mail-train loco that ran from Los Angeles to Chicago. Wonder if its whistle toots, "Hello, sailor!" *Courtesy MTH-RailKing*

Contents

Acknowledgments

The authors wish to acknowledge the help and cooperation of Susan Childers, curator, Carail Museum, Detroit, Michigan; Mitch Kuhn, camera assistant; Mike Moore, Toys and Trains Hobby Shop (Lionel); Elaine Silets, Huff & Puff Industries; David Newsted; John Hetreed; and Stan Roy.

Introduction

The era of modern toy trains began at the market's nadir. By 1969, Lionel—virtually the only game in town—had fallen on its own sword and existed only as a logo steeped in red ink. In continuous production since 1901, Lionel plants shut down and their remaining train sets attracted dust bunnies on dealers' shelves.

As the war in Vietnam raged, so too did protesters. Hippies tuned out and the toy market was awash in war, space, fright, and otherwise gruesome toys. Commands were uttered in robotic voices and diecast cars zipped through plastic "fun loops" on rec room floors. Child-safety and morality groups rushed into the toy market, demanding reform and forcing manufacturers to pull war-and-gore toys off the shelves at the expense of the bottom line. As the 1970s dawned, many toy companies became financially vulnerable.

Two phenomena saved toy trains: corporate conglomerates and demanding collectors. At a time when railroads themselves were also a faded shell of their past glory, kids were equally jaded about anything on tracks. But large segments of corporate America were cash-rich: one of those segments was the cereal industry. Cereal companies loved kids. Kids played with toys. Spreading the corporate umbrella to include toy companies seemed natural. As their competition fanned out, dragging stunned toy companies back to their corporate caves, General Mills' hunter-gatherers netted Rainbow Crafts, Regal Toy, Chad Valley, Kenner, and Parker Brothers. They also tossed a 3 1/2 percent royalty on annual sales to Lionel for use

Marx Trains has a large following among tinplate modelers who enjoy the toylike look and jewel-color finish of the manufacturer's rolling stock and locomotives.
Courtesy Marx Trains

of their logo and to determine if any profit could be squeezed from dusty inventories.

As they pushed a few colorful diesels out the door with their 1970 catalog, General Mills discovered the toy train collector. Kids were elbowed aside by middle-aged enthusiasts bent on reliving their youth by collecting the bits and pieces that remained and building clubs such as the Train Collectors Association and the Toy Train Operating Society. The Lionel Toy Division of General Mills' Model Products Corporation, a part of "Fundimensions," found themselves with an actual demand for toy trains, and they set out to fill it.

The story of Lionel's rebirth in the modern toy train era is not a unique tale. From the dim and distant past, the sleeping Gods of Market Share stirred and nudged a few entrepreneurs into action. In place of such faded names as Carlisle & Finch, Ives, Dorfan, Girard, Hafner, and American Flyer ("The Brand That Refuses to Die"), came Jerry Williams, building reproductions of Ives and Lionel Standard Gauge trains. He expanded his garage shop into a full line of O gauge motive power and rolling stock requiring considerable factory space. Williams' young assistant, Mike Wolf, spun off his own company, Mike's Train House, which begat RailKing and roared into the marketplace with exquisite Korean-built models.

Meanwhile, Maury Klein started out selling O gauge track and ended up moving superdetailed models out of his shop at low prices. Weaver Models bridged the scale and toy train markets with great products that looked good on both two-rail and three-rail track. And, of course, the clever, tinny little trains of Louis Marx are still available with fresh designs from Jim and Debby Flynn's Marx Trains, Inc.

As if the tinplate market were not enough for collectors, kids, and operators, toy trains have embraced a new gauge variously described as G gauge, No. 1 gauge, Large Scale, 22 1/2-inch scale, and 45 millimeter, depending on the manufacturer. These huge trains roll through gardens and snowdrifts, as well as on indoor pikes. They also represent the hobby's fastest-growing segment. Of course, within each brand, there are variations in scale, track, and just about everything else—just enough to drive operators mad. Nothing ever really changes.

Today, Lionel is healthy under yet another management group and is moving its manufacturing offshore to join the other manufacturers and maintain its competitive edge. The hobby is once again a terrific horse race in a field of quality-driven companies. Today's toy train hobbyist (and his or her pocketbook) is the recipient of their concentrated attention. Computer technology, casting and color processes, marketing, and distribution have all changed since postwar golden age tinplate trains first brought grins to kids on Christmas morning. Incredible realism exists alongside truly silly fantasy—and there is a market for both.

At train shows today, kids rooted in place by the rock and roll of big, noisy toy trains operated by adults in striped engineer caps offer a glimpse of things to come. Kids are returning to toy trains, viewing these railroads not as remembrances of the past, but as challenges of the now and future. Modern toy trains no longer rely on the ups and downs of their predecessors. With their vast array of electronics and computer-driven features, the new trains are the most complex toys available today. They are ready for the next generation to take the throttle.

Lionel's popular *General*, with its diamond stack and protruding cowcatcher, hauled many nineteenth-century freight and passenger trains in the late 1950s during the "Western" craze on television. It popped up again throughout the 1970s and 1980s in a variety of liveries, from the blue Baltimore & Ohio 8315 of 1983, to the all-black-with-gold-trim Western & Atlantic of 1977. On the inside track is the shiny Rock Island & Peoria 1980 model, complete with a mountain mural on its wood-hauling tender. *Courtesy Carail Museum, Detroit, Michigan*

Lionel Resurrected: The Grain Grinders Take Over

By 1970, American railroads had been flattened by draconian interstate commerce laws. As the airlines sucked away passenger service, thousands of miles of interstate highways teemed with trucks that cut deeply into freight service. Toy trains were in the same boat. In 1971, Louis Marx cashed in on his overseas plants to post earnings of $67 million. When he died in 1982, the last of the toy train moguls was gone. Marx's former company, like those of Joshua Lionel Cowen and A.C. Gilbert, slid downhill on greased rails.

At the time, Lionel was a logo on kids' leisurewear. Ron Saypol, who had married Cowen's granddaughter, created Lionel Leisure stores. If the product was not selling, at least his timing was good. Corporations were looking far afield of their core competencies for opportunities to diversify, and forming "corporate conglomerates" in the process. Mammoth cereal corporations bought toy companies that were struggling amidst a public backlash against store shelves full of war-and-gore toys.

To handle their toy and game acquisitions, General Mills created the "Fundimensions" group and the Model Products Corporation. While such companies as Parker Brothers, Kenner, and Regal Toy fell into General Mills' net, the cereal maker also scooped up use of the Lionel logo and current inventories for a 3 1/2 percent royalty on annual sales. Crates of parts were opened, tools and dies were inventoried, and a marketing plan was drawn up.

The marketplace was a *tabula rasa*—a blank page. Kids of 1970 could not care less about frowsy old steam engines, now gutted husks lined up nose to tail on scrap tracks. Prototype railroad motive power had become a rainbow collection of colorful diesels. Fortunately for Lionel, technology offered new ways to achieve brilliant colors and lettering schemes. Thanks to thermal ("electrocal") and interchangeable color pads ("tampo") lettering methods, and colored plastic in pellet and liquid form, toy trains could have their own rainbow of hues.

Somewhat-stripped Santa Fe Alcos and NW2 switchers began rolling out of Lionel's

In early 1971, Fundimensions began pushing proven winners back into the market. The Electro-Motive F Series, first made famous by Lionel's signature 1948 Santa Fe F3, was reissued starting with the 8363-64 Baltimore & Ohio A-A. This powered and dummy pair operated with a single motor. It featured neither Magne-Traction nor an electric horn. *Courtesy Carail Museum, Detroit, Michigan*

In 1970, Lionel blew the dust off postwar plastic shells and recalled the NW2 diesel switcher to duty. The reintroduction of the 1965 model helped lead Lionel back onto the mainline. *Courtesy Carail Museum, Detroit, Michigan*

shop in Mount Clemens, Michigan, followed by a GP9 in Illinois Central livery and a Canadian National GP7. The only difference between the two GP locos was a snap-on fan shroud on the roof of the GP9. These were the trains kids saw every day, and a flurry of road names was added. Also benefiting from these new color-application technologies was a bevy of boxcars, the 9400 series that featured not just the major Class 1 railroad liveries, but shortlines as well.

Initially, Lionel cut costs by dropping Magne-Traction in favor of "Pullmor" rubber tires to achieve grip. Hollow electrical pick-up rollers that were substituted for solid rollers were later recalled when it was discovered that the center rails on the tinplate track deeply scored them. To further cut overhead, Lionel also dusted off old dies, among them two 2-4-2 steam engines in plastic and cast metal. As Lionel elbowed its way back into the market, these were their only steam offerings.

In 1973, Lionel announced a revival of their classic F3 diesel streamliner, rolling out sets in Baltimore & Ohio and Canadian Pacific liveries. These F3 engines featured the Type 1 body style, the first of what would become Lionel-MPC's six variations on the window, porthole, and louver arrangement. The announcement of these engines and car sets awakened a sleeping giant that became the driving force in Lionel's production and marketing initiatives—adult toy train collectors and operators.

The Train Collectors Association (TCA), started in 1954, and the Toy Train Operating

Society, which came into being in 1966, had affiliated clubs and divisions across the country. Club members, who had been running the wheels off their collectible prewar and postwar trains, started buying up these new offerings. In 1971, Lionel had produced a car exclusively for the TCA. Designed by train collector and former Disney animator Ward Kimball, the 6464-1971 car decorated with Disney characters sold out its run of 1,500 units. These collectors had deep pockets, but were also finicky and discerning. They demanded new products as well as reissues of the old chestnuts. One model, rushed out the door as a collectible in 1973, was a GP7 commemorating the fiftieth anniversary of GM's Electro-Motive Division (EMD). Its run of 9,000 units quickly sold through, proving the value of the collectors' buying power.

Lionel designers and marketers hit another bonanza when EMD sliced the nose of the standard GP7 in half lengthwise to produce the "new" GP20. In addition, new alliances between trucking companies and railroads also impacted Lionel, who turned out intermodal rolling stock units featuring trucking logos on truck trailers loaded onto flatcars. The possibilities were endless.

From 1973 to 1975, the 8352 GP20 was a standby workhorse. Because diesels were cheaper to build than steam engines and were based on contemporary trains, Lionel-MPC created several of the boxy locos as they gained market momentum. *Courtesy Carail Museum, Detroit, Michigan*

Produced in 1976, Lionel's No. 8558 Milwaukee Road version of the EP5 was a fairly accurate reproduction of the original, but it had four-wheel trucks instead of the correct six wheels. The centenary allowed power to reach the single motor from overhead wires. *Courtesy Carail Museum, Detroit, Michigan*

As the 1970s matured, so did the confidence of Lionel designers. In 1974, they introduced their first new diesel locomotive not based on any previous postwar design: the U36, or "U-Boat," whose prototype was built by General Electric. The 1976 version of this heavy hauler was decorated in red, white, and blue centennial colors and hooked to a string of boxcars, each representing one of the 13 original colonies.

Still, Lionel-MPC did manage a couple of duds during this heady time. While "Tru-Track" featured more ties, a T-shaped rail, and rubber roadbed, the company, in their zeal to crank out a more prototypical look, overlooked the fact that Tru-Track's aluminum rails would eliminate the power of Magne-Traction, affecting both older locos and newer ones that incorporated this feature. In addition, a 1977 reissue of the classic GG1 was also received

with indifference by adult enthusiasts who, if they didn't look askance at its ragged castings, discovered that its nylon gears quickly wore out. A black Penn Central version, with its "mating worms" logo, represented the bankrupt 1976 merger of the New York Central and the Pennsylvania Railroad—a bad omen for the time. Lionel would trot out the GG1 again and again, trying to get it right.

Nostalgia-driven collectors were also discontented with the flood of diesels. They wanted steamers. But the suits in General Mills' corporate towers wanted all their toy divisions to meet profit quotas and steam locos cost considerably more to produce with their complex castings and details. Lionel had to make do with the dies they had uncrated. In 1972, they tested the waters with the 8206 "small" Hudson, adding their new Sound of Steam, a whistle, and Pullmor rubber tires in

In 1976, Lionel issued their 1776 Seaboard Coast Line U36B in red, white, and blue, as well as a series of 13 boxcars, each representing one of the original colonies. It ran on one motor and had electric pickup in only one truck. *Courtesy John Hetreed Collection*

place of Magne-Traction. But the soft edges of the old dies limited its acceptance, as did off-center driving wheels that gave it a ducklike waddle down the mainline. A unique engine did emerge that year, however. Although the 8209 Docksider tank locomotive did look like engines that hauled log trains along the Pacific Coast, it proved a modest success as a yard goat.

Once Lionel committed to adding steam power to their line, designers resurrected several more old dies, including the 1964 "small" Hudson 8600, with its 4-6-4 wheel configuration stuffed under a Berkshire boiler casting. Lionel also tried to dress up the steam line with color. The silver-and-green Southern Crescent Hudson came out in 1977 with gold striping and a set of matching 9500 passenger cars. Even more gaudy steamers were on the boards for the approaching 1980s.

Even though the 1977 GG1 was a snooze, other electric locomotives called "motors"

To get some idea of the compression of Lionel's O gauge offerings, this 1977 4-6-4 8702 small Hudson model of the Southern *Crescent Limited* is paired with the full-scale 1401 Southern Crescent as a prototypically correct 4-8-2. The Southern never ran any 4-6-4s, but the 4-8-2 was built to handle passenger trains in hilly country. Both locos are painted Virginia Green with gold striping. *Courtesy Carail Museum, Detroit, Michigan*

were uncrated and reissued. The EP5 was shopped out in 1975 in Pennsylvania Railroad colors. It ran well and, like the GG1, its pantographs could take power from overhead wire. Other road names followed, including the Great Northern, which actually had no EP5s on its roster. E33 "rectifier" motors, with their single pantograph and boxy looks, were added to the electric ranks in 1976. The blue-and-yellow Virginian, a reasonable facsimile of its 3,300-horsepower prototype, ran well at the head of freight consists.

Lionel also expanded the line from electric motors to include passenger cars based on diesel-powered prototypes built by the Budd Company for commuter lines without electrification. Lionel revived their 1956 version of

these shiny aluminum trains in 1977, and in 1978 added Amtrak markings. These rail diesel cars (RDCs) ran well and added commuter service to a layout without the need to string real or simulated overhead wire for a prototype appearance.

The first 10 years of Lionel's diesel and electric output as part of General Mills was impressive, and 1980 was commemorated with the trundling out of a brick of a locomotive: a virtually exact copy of Lionel's postwar Fairbanks-Morse TrainMaster. Its brutish, twin-motor pulling power (topped only by the GG1), simulated six-wheel trucks for tight curves, and a variety of colorful road schemes made it a winner and gave collectors hope that Lionel management was, finally, on the right track.

15

Jerry Williams and Williams Electric Trains

Just as Joshua Lionel Cowen shaped Lionel, Williams Electric Trains strongly reflects the agenda of its founder and owner, Jerry Williams. Williams Electric Trains has no archive. There are no cardboard boxes in a back room, no lovingly preserved relics of the early years perched on shelves. Every move is a move forward, and there is no looking back. Apparently, this single-minded approach worked for Williams as he elbowed his way into the toy train market in 1976.

A transplanted Californian who was shuttled eastward to Maryland at a tender age, Williams developed his gift for mathematics at Washington, D.C.'s American University and the Johns Hopkins University Applied Physics Laboratory before going on to work as a data analyst. He quit all that to make toy trains.

Williams enjoyed collecting trains and became a member of the Train Collectors Association (TCA) in 1968. By the mid-1970s, most of the very early Lionel, Dorfan, Ives, and Carlisle & Finch products that remained had been snapped up by the folks with the deepest pockets. So, in 1969, Williams and a partner created Classic Models Corporation, and began cranking out Standard Gauge locos and rolling stock that collectors could actually run withot affecting their market value.

Williams' pioneering work assumed that collectors would at least like to own a reproduction of a bygone locomotive, since the originals were becoming increasingly rare and expensive. Of course, purists and rivet-counters voiced objections to "fake" collectibles. In the face of this sentiment, Williams decided that his look-alike models just didn't go far enough. He wanted "look-exactly-alikes."

Choosing the rare O gauge Model 1694 Lionel-Ives electric as his first challenge, Williams borrowed a repainted (and less valuable) original, stripped it, sent the parts' dimensions to die makers, and had 300 sets of the 1694 parts run off. The locomotives debuted at the 1972 TCA Convention and were promptly snapped up.

Williams used the profits from the venture to create his first Standard Gauge copy: the Lionel No. 9 electric loco. Once again, he stripped a No. 9 engine and used what bits he could from the 1694 dies to save money. Soon, huge cartons of parts began arriving at his home. He needed help. Neighbors and local kids were drafted to put together subassemblies. As the legend goes, one of those kids was a 12-year-old named Mike Wolf, who was starting a career in the toy train business by spending Saturdays in Jerry Williams' basement, hooking together parts of a Lionel reproduction.

The Williams No. 9 electric went on sale a year after the 1694's success. Before they

Limited runs of Williams hand-built brass locomotives arrived in 1984. The New York Central Hudson scale model was a stunning creation, rivaling Lionel's 700E diecast engine of 1937. It was offered with five heavyweight "Madison" passenger cars. These models, though they could run on standard three-rail track, could no longer be considered "toy trains." Courtesy Williams Electric Trains

were even out the door, Williams was planning to reproduce Lionel's big green No. 381, the heavy-hauling No. 408 S-Motor electric, and the No. 8 trolley. By 1975, business was moving along briskly. Then, Williams sent out his first promotional brochure, opening the floodgates. During this time, he was still working as a data analyst by day. When the crunch came, Williams chose toy trains and never looked back.

By 1977, Williams was turning out both O gauge and Standard Gauge copies of Lionel products, as well as spare parts, under the company name Williams Reproductions. In 1980, the company moved into

a newly constructed facility located in Columbia, Maryland.

Williams Reproductions reached its first crisis in 1980, when they were stuck with a considerable backlog of unsold Standard Gauge passenger cars and had to job them out to volume dealers at a discount. The move angered quite a few old customers who had bought the cars at full price. The experience soured Jerry Williams on the further market potential for Standard Gauge reproductions, and led him to concentrate exclusively on the O gauge tinplate market. With that decision, Jerry Williams joined the competition that was emerging on Lionel's unprotected flanks.

Lionel also put all their bait in the water to appeal to collectors with rolling stock. Three interesting attempts best illustrate their efforts. From 1976 through 1978, Lionel churned out a series of "collector cars" that would have had Joshua Lionel Cowen revving up in his grave. Each boxcar in the "Tobacco Road" series depicted a brand of cigarettes, cigars, or pipe tobacco. Cowen's rule had been to never place on any Lionel car any logo representing any product that was bad for kids. His pleasantly naïve concept was trod on over and over in the 1980s, as vat cars toted Miller Lite Beer and boxcars were loaded with Coors beer and Black Label whisky.

In 1977, Lionel introduced a series of "Hi-Cube" boxcars. These standard "40-foot" cars were built up to 18 scale inches higher with large doors and no catwalks on the roof. Besides bringing out standard road names, Lionel decorated a string of cars with Disney characters and scenes from Disney films. The idea was to collect them as they were issued between 1977 and 1978.

By 1980, collectors could also buy a set of big-league sports cars, with each 9700 boxcar

In 1979, Fundimensions rolled out a series of Fairbanks-Morse TrainMaster diesels. This Jersey Central Lines version was dual motored with Magne-Traction. Earlier TrainMaster plastic shells had a tendency to crack around the screw holes that connected to the metal frame; this 1986 model had reinforced screw holes. *Courtesy Stan Roy Collection*

An earlier 1978 version of the popular 4-4-2 Atlantic had basically the same engine shell as the postwar 2037 model, except for a reworked boiler. These locos were the backbone of the Lionel-MPC steamer line; this one received Sound of Steam and has been gussied up with fine detailing and a square-back tender. *Courtesy Carail Museum, Detroit, Michigan*

commemorating a sports association. The series will always remain incomplete, however, since the National Football League declined to join the other leagues. In addition, some collectors complained because many of the cars were sold in sets, and to buy the one you wanted, you had to fork over cash for the others, as well.

While Lionel groped about for a market in the 1970s, the competition was virtually nowhere to be found, except for a number of small shops that had set up business in the 1960s to make spare parts as Lionel's fortunes skidded. While kids abandoned toy trains for war and gore, outer space, and autos to race, maturing Lionel collectors had

Diecast diesels designed for three-rail track were a major part of Williams' O gauge offerings as the line expanded in 1981. This scale-dimension SD45 in Erie Lackawana livery has authentic six-wheel trucks and wire handrails. Its couplers were compatible with Lionel or MTH. At $200, the dual-motored heavy hauler was a bargain. *Courtesy Williams Electric Trains*

two options: operate their collectibles and run the risk of diminishing their value, or store the trains on shelves to gather dust as their desirability grew.

Into this deteriorating situation stepped Jerry Williams, a data analyst and member of the TCA. By 1971, toy train collectors and operators were scavenging estate sales and flea markets for bits and pieces of Lionel trains to keep their aging tinplate running. Williams thought that he would offer a replica—the very rare 1694 Lionel-Ives transition electric in O gauge—to TCA members. In 1972 he did just that and sold all 300. With that success under his belt, Williams raised his sights to old Lionel Standard Gauge locomotives such as the Model 9 electric—another relative rarity. To help him assemble

Versions of this Southern Pacific *Daylight* 4-8-4 are very valuable collectors' items. This one shares the same small drivers and trucks as the Norfolk & Western J-Class steamer, and should share the title of one of Lionel's most elegant steam engines. This 1983 version features Sound of Steam and Magne-Traction, as well as smoke from the stack and "steam" from the cylinders. *Courtesy Mike Moore Collection*

the parts in his garage shop, he hired a 12-year-old kid named Mike Wolf to join his team of friends and part-time housewives. Wolf would become a volatile force in the toy train industry, but not before the garage shop blossomed into a profitable business called Williams Reproductions.

Of course, the garage entrepreneurs weren't even blips on Lionel's radar. The word from General Mills was, "Crank it up a notch. Get into these collectors' pockets! You can even spend money to do it."

Lionel's steam fleet benefited most from this burst of largess. Steamwise, Lionel's first 10 years under General Mills were a bit lame. The little Columbia 2-4-2 utility locos and their smaller cousin, the Porter 2-4-0 (a postwar Lionel Scout cast in plastic), were joined

A fine old Lionel classic was revived in 1984: the 6-8-6 S-2 turbine in Pennsylvania Brunswick Green with a graphite-gray smoke box. It carried Sound of Steam and was powered by a Berkshire motor powering a small set of drivers, which irritated collectors. *Courtesy Carail Museum, Detroit, Michigan*

Right: Williams joined Mike Wolf in 1984, having brass models built at Samhongsa in Korea. Williams' earliest brass locos were the Pennsy's slight Pacific and the New York Central Hudson. The parts were created in Korea and then shipped to Williams for final assembly. The steamers were built with DC motors for both two-rail scale-model operators and AC motors for flanged-wheel, three-rail operation. *Courtesy Williams Electric Trains*

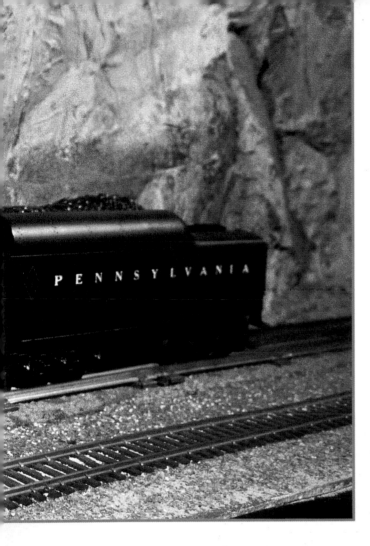

by a 4-4-2 Atlantic, a body type that would see considerable use in the coming years. Except for 0-4-0 switchers, the rest of the line was made up of the "small" Hudsons in various garbs. So, when the parent company sent out the edict to get into the collectors' wallets, cost be (somewhat) damned, Lionel tested the market in 1977 with a reissue of the gaily colored *General* 4-4-0 American-type locomotive originally designed in the late 1950s. The *General* was rolled out again in 1980, its diamond stack and "Western" appearance making it a popular seller that would be resurrected through the years.

One of Lionel's most beautiful locomotives, the 8309 Southern Pacific *Daylight*, was also recalled to duty with a full load of features buried under its bright orange paint.

This FP5 was designed by Williams in 1984 and released in 1985. These diecast Amfleet locos were built for use with Amtrak passenger cars already being made by Fundimensions' Lionel. It operated on 31-inch O gauge track. Later versions employed dual flywheel motors and True-Sounds. *Courtesy Williams Electric Trains*

Berkshire 2-8-4 locomotives—the most ubiquitous of postwar designs—rolled out in garish Chessie System yellow edging and tender art, alongside a two-tone gray version with "elephant ear" smoke deflectors.

As the 1980s progressed, the cranks turned and the gears hummed at the Mount Clemens plant. Even the monster hit of 1946, the Pennsylvania S-2 steam turbine loco, was resurrected as the model 8404. The 6-8-6 was

The very first American G scale prototype from LGB was this nineteenth-century 2-6-0 Mogul introduced in 1984. While it is more "American" than the little 0-4-0 "Stainz," it still reflects the European love of color and brass. *Courtesy LGB*

started up with a Brunswick green boiler and graphite-gray smoke box, striped with white trim, complemented with a 2046-type water scoop tender, and numbered 6200.

But the profits were still not flowing in fast enough to soften the hearts of the General Mills bean counters. For a cereal company accustomed to a predictable flow of cash as boxes of puffed and sweetened grain flew off the shelves and onto breakfast tables, the toy market turned out to be a hit-or-miss affair that wasn't worth the trouble. As a cost-saving attempt, they boxed up Lionel and sent it to Mexico—a *maquiladora*, owned by Americans and staffed by Mexicans—to take advantage of less expensive labor. But the learning curve demanded by General Mills and the quality standards expected by collectors were not met by the move, and a stream of Lionel refugees traipsed back to Mount Clemens after the failed experiment.

By this time, General Mills wanted out of the toy business and, in 1985, cut loose the companies one by one, dissolving the conglomerate. Lionel was folded into Kenner-Parker, who was clueless concerning toy trains or their market. Once again, the old storage crates were dug out and another end loomed after 15 years of production.

Then millionaire collector Richard Kughn stepped in and bought the company.

Williams' brass models included rolling stock as well. This 1992 New York Central caboose looks very authentic except for the tinplate couplers. The sharp edges, immaculate paint jobs, and crisp details gave Williams freight cars considerable panache—for $140 a pop. *Courtesy Williams Electric Trains*

Rescue and Total War: The Kughn Years Begin

R ichard Kughn saved Lionel from another trip to the dumpster and, in the process, burnished the grand old logo to a bright shine. This he managed with marketing savvy, the help of good people, and a charmingly ruthless attitude toward weeding out the competition.

A visit to Kughn's Carail Museum in Detroit reveals a great deal about the man. From the outside, the undistinguished concrete building squats on its site like a bunker, giving no hint of what's beyond the walls. Once inside, visitors are surrounded by a compilation of collections scattered in rooms, lining the walls, and even filling niches where museum administration takes place. Beautifully restored antique automobiles glisten as if new, while shelf upon shelf of Lionel trains march toward the ceilings. There seems to be one of just about everything Lionel ever built. Four white rooms are dedicated to specific years of production: 1998, 1999, 2000, and 2001. Carail helps pay its way by renting out the main room for banquets and parties. In that room, round tables sit like white lily pads in the midst of a huge layout designed and maintained by staffer John Wetzel. On the layout, there's a mix of Standard Gauge Lionel antiques; prewar, postwar, and contemporary O gauge Lionel trains; accessories; and assorted buildings and scenes of all kinds. Courteous, hard-working, and very loyal employees staff the whole operation. In this hallowed place, the sun rises and sets on the Lionel name. Mention the name

Mike Wolf or his company, Mike's Train House, and all conversation dies as the air temperature drops 40 degrees.

"We don't mention either of those names around here," you'll be informed.

Kughn's tenure at Lionel's helm was marked by an obsession with quality and an attitude about the competition that recalled Joshua Lionel Cowen's disdain for those "other people" who also made toy trains.

Williams began their Crown Line of fine brass locomotives and rolling stock in 1986. This L-1 Pennsylvania Railroad light Mikado 2-8-2 built in 1987 is typical of their mid-size steamers. *Courtesy Williams Electric Trains*

The first steam engine from Richard Kughn's Lionel Trains in 1987 was this Rock Island Northern 4-8-4. This was Lionel's first true Northern-type boiler and, once announced, was eagerly awaited. Unfortunately, after many delays, dealers received stock that had defective armatures in some, rough castings on all, and a plastic coupler on the tender. Lionel did turn around complaints and the later models pulled their weight. Today, some collectors still call this model an "AWS" ("Ain't Worth S**t"). *Courtesy Mike Moore Collection*

The 18300 Pennsylvania Railroad GG1 of 1987 was the usual dual-motored electric with Magne-Traction and operating pantographs, but it was painted bronze. The locomotive was tarted up and matched with an equally bronzed porthole caboose for the express purpose of hauling the really silly, open-window bullion cars. *Courtesy Stan Roy Collection*

29

In one corner of the large banquet room is a garbage can filled with junk and topped with a broken, prewar Lionel loco and a couple of cars. It is actually a planned display recounting the day when Kughn, at age seven, retrieved his first Lionel train from a garbage can and fixed it up well enough to run again. That's exactly what he did to Lionel the company after General Mills fled the field.

Although Kughn made most of his millions as a builder, in real estate, and collecting companies, at heart he's a train guy. Even his approach to his hobbies takes on a grand scale. To fatten up his collection, he purchased Madison Hardware, a former Manhattan Lionel dealership, and shipped its contents to Detroit, where he selected the best items for his walls, cases, shelves, and layouts.

When Kughn learned from Arthur Piesner and other toy executives at General Mills in 1986 that Kenner-Parker—formerly a part of Fundimensions, General Mills' defunct conglomerate—wanted to dump Lionel, he came up with the cash for a buyout of the Lionel and American Flyer logos and assets. The original idea was that Kughn would get to wear the engineer's hat, blow the whistle, and pay the bills, while former General Mills executives ran the show. It didn't entirely work out that way.

Piesner's people wanted to go head-to-head with Mattel and Hasbro, creating action figures and Hot Wheels rip-offs bearing the valuable Lionel logo. Their efforts met with profound apathy at the stores. Kughn, meanwhile, was faced with unsold Lionel products, a damaged distribution system, and the need to put new products on the market without spending any money. In short order, Piesner's name was scraped off the office door and Nick DeGrazia's was painted on. Kughn fell back on the knowledge he gained running 81 companies under Kughn Enterprises. He took over Lionel Trains, Inc., and firmly set its wheels back on the track. DeGrazia became a cheerleader for whatever came out the door and a target of customer wrath for whatever flopped.

Lionel Trains, Inc., needed a big opening gun to announce Lionel's return. They chose a Rock Island 4-8-4 Northern numbered 5100, a brutish heavy hauler offering the full range of Lionel features: Magne-Traction, Sound of Steam, a whistle, and smoke, not only from the stack, but as cylinder emissions as well. The first castings were ragged, but were improved. A plastic dummy coupler on the tender was replaced with a working version. Lionel was actually listening to the collectors' complaints.

Joining the Rock Island steamer in 1987 was an 18300 bronze GG1 with matching caboose designed to haul bullion boxcars. Its nonprototype color scheme was typical of the philosophy of collectibles for their own sake rather than reproductions of real prototypes, a concept that would spread like a rash throughout the Lionel line.

In addition to the T-1 Reading 4-8-4 released in 1989, Lionel built a T-1 boiler loco number 2101 in Chessie System colors, complete with the latest RailSounds in 1991. *Courtesy Carail Museum, Detroit, Michigan*

The wave of 1987 offerings continued to roll as Lionel Trains, Inc., ventured into new waters with a line of big G scale trains. Garden railroading had caught on in the United States during the cash-rich 1980s, when LGB began offering big, sturdy trains that could run comfortably outdoors on weatherproof track. The locomotives and cars were obviously based on European prototypes, but the idea of running trains through backyard gardens quickly gained popularity. Lionel jumped into the market, first with cartoonlike 0-4-0 locos and later with big American diesels. But they were not alone, as Bachmann and Aristo-Craft, the latter being the largest dealer of Lionel OO gauge

products, also joined in the competition. Lionel's launch fell short, and though the line continued for almost 10 years, by 1996 the trains were selling at knockdown prices to clear out inventories. But, like many bright Lionel ideas, the G scale concept was shelved for the time being, not buried.

The next watershed year for Lionel Trains, Inc., was 1989. As the line of locomotives, rolling stock, and accessories reestablished the company in the toy train marketplace, Richard Kughn took note of a number of small companies that were turning out spare parts and replicas of Lionel products. Many of them were selling their products out of their vans at

LGB:
Big-Train Pioneers

Many garden layouts in the United States feature an alpine theme. Some garden railroaders choose such a setting because of the European G scale trains that were available before American-style prototypes made their appearance. The RhB Ge 4/4 electric loco is the current backbone of the Swiss Rhatische Bahn. LGB's model looks right at home in the snow and offers many electronic features.
Courtesy LGB

The world's first "G scale" train was created in 1968, but the history of LGB goes way back to 1881, when Ernst Paul Lehmann founded a small toymaking company in Brandenburg, Germany.

Lehmann had a keen eye for new ideas, and his "patent" toys, including the honking Tut Tut auto and flying Ikarus airplane, soon gave Ernst Paul Lehmann Patentwerk a worldwide reputation for innovation. Lehmann's cousin, Johannes Richter, joined the company in 1921 and moved his family to Nuremberg. After World War II, Richter and his sons, Eberhard and Wolfgang, rebuilt the family firm. Twenty years later, in 1968, the sons introduced the family's boldest invention ever: LGB, or "The Big Train."

Ernst Paul Lehmann Patentwerk is still family owned, with Eberhard and Wolfgang's sons, Johannes and Rolf, at the helm. The LGB family also includes dedicated em-ploy-ees in Nuremberg and at LGB of America in San Diego, California. Today, LGB crafts trains using the latest in computer-aided design techniques, precision machining processes, and robotic production. Their catalog features more than 600 G scale train products.

LGB's creation, G scale, utilizes track machined from virgin brass and mounted on composite ties. The trains themselves are built from weather- and impact-resistant materials. Gearboxes are sealed, protected from dirt and moisture. These incredibly durable engines are at home outside in any weather, even snow. In fact, snowplows are available for clearing the tracks, just like with prototypes.

This 1989 B-6 Pennsylvania Railroad switcher was the first Lionel locomotive to use RailSounds. A remake of the 1939 227/701 scale model built for T-rail track, it also featured smoke and correct arch bar trucks on the stretch slope-back tender. Today, this model is a valued collector piece. *Courtesy Stan Roy Collection*

toy train swap meets. The majority were start-ups left over from Lionel's Fundimensions days, when pounding out products to meet the bottom line left no budget to beat up on mom-and-pop shops bagging spare parts in their garages.

From Kughn's point of view, all this free-booting had to stop. A blizzard of letters threatening legal action dropped on the toy train companies. No one had pockets deep enough to fight Lionel's lawyers, so the competition

virtually dried up. Everyone, that is, except Mike's Train House. Mike Wolf never got a letter. He got a phone call.

Wolf had achieved success building Lionel Standard Gauge replicas after purchasing the tooling and rights to do so from Williams Reproductions. Through his association with Jerry Williams, Wolf had also contracted Samhongsa (roughly translated, "future oriented") in Korea to build the models to very high standards.

A model that would find its way into other manufacturers' lineups 10 years later, the Pennsylvania Railroad E6 Atlantic *Lindbergh Special* dating back to 1910 was another Williams brass classic of 1989. *Courtesy Williams Electric Trains*

Lionel also wanted to reduce their labor costs and raise manufacturing standards by building trains overseas. Dan Cooney, a Lionel chief operating officer, contacted Samhongsa in October 1986 to negotiate a manufacturing deal. Se Young Lee, Samhongsa's director, turned down the deal, preferring to maintain the relationship with MTH. When Wolf heard about Lionel's offer, he called Cooney and suggested they talk about a three-way deal. Cooney turned down the MTH offer. The

whole idea, after all, was to muscle MTH out of business. In 1987, Cooney tried Samhongsa again and got the same answer. Again, Wolf suggested a partnership and was sent packing. In July 1987, the phone rang at MTH and Wolf was finally invited by Cooney to visit Lionel's Mount Clemens, Michigan, headquarters to open talks.

Lionel asked Wolf to come on board for five years as a design consultant and to build new products using his Samhongsa connection.

Mike Wolf and the Rise of His Train House

Mike Wolf began his career in the toy train business by assembling latch couplers on copies of Lionel's No. 9 electric locomotive for $1.50 an hour in Jerry Williams' basement. He was 12 years old and that money was good for a kid back in 1970. Most of his coworkers were teenagers—some of them were even girls.

Wolf was valued by Williams as one of the hardest workers in the budding cottage industry called Williams Reproductions. At one point, his dropping grades in high-school English prompted Jerry to ask his wife, Sally, to tutor young Wolf, rather than risk losing one of his best employees to the rigors of academia.

In 1978, Wolf graduated from high school and continued on with his job, by now earning $7.50 an hour working for Williams. When it came time for college, he switched from the University of Maryland to Howard Community College so he could be closer to his work. The job and the knowledge he was gaining about the business had become an obsession. Eventually, as he commuted from Towson State University—where he earned a degree in business administration—to Williams' shop, Wolf rose to become Williams' second in command.

In time, Wolf realized he could create his own business. He had experienced success selling Standard Gauge replacement parts, and when Jerry Williams decided to drop his Standard Gauge line, Wolf stepped in, gambling $40,000 to purchase the Standard Gauge inventory and the rights to Williams' dies from 1970 through 1973. Mike's father, Paul Wolf, cashed in his retirement savings to help his son buy the tooling outright.

Mike's Train House had a bumpy start, with Wolf paying off his debts to Jerry Williams and his father. But in 1985, Wolf contacted Se Young Lee, a representative of Samhongsa, a Korean model toy manufacturer. Although Lee had come to the United States to get business from Jerry Williams, he and Wolf developed a business relationship that became a friendship that affected Wolf's career to the present day.

Lee headed back to Korea with a job to produce the tooling for the Lionel Standard Gauge 214 refrigerator car and the Model 200 boxcar—at his own expense. This act of trust and the excellent quality of the products that returned from Korea cemented their personal and business relationship. They established a direct, state-of-the-art (for 1985) communications link between Korea and Mike's company via fax machines.

As Wolf's business grew, he added the 400E locomotive to his Standard Gauge roster and leased 4,000 square feet of manufacturing

In 1937, the Reading Railroad climbed on the streamliner bandwagon with the Crusader. In 1999, MTH unveiled its version of the stainless-steel locomotive and its four-car passenger set. Created for RailKing O gauge, the diecast 4-6-2 Pacific-type carries the usual "Proto" package of sounds and systems. It is designed for 31-inch curves, while Weaver's scale-model brass version of the Crusader requires a 54-inch radius—and a few more dollars.
Courtesy MTH-RailKing

room from Williams Reproductions, now located in Columbia, Maryland. Then, he drove to about 30 train shows a year in a van that burned what he later claimed to be a gallon of motor oil every 60 miles.

Then, in 1987, everything changed. Richard Kughn, real-estate developer and collector of companies, cars, and toy trains, bought Lionel from Kenner-Parker, who had inherited the line when General Mills cut the toymaker loose from its conglomerate. Kughn immediately set about to establish Lionel as the *only* maker of Lionel products. A phalanx of lawyers bearing a flurry of lawsuits was dispatched to the small fringe businesses that frequented the train show circuit with home-cooked Lionel look-alikes. This legal savaging, however, featured one interesting anomaly: MTH never received a cease-and-desist letter. A strange bond was in the making.

This Chicago & North Western 4-4-2 Atlantic is actually a stretch Columbia built over an AC/DC can motor for the 1990 market. The new can motors were more reliable than the skew-wound armature motors that began fading out. Atlantic types could haul freight or passenger consists without looking out of place.
Courtesy Carail Museum, Detroit, Michigan

T-1, No. 2100, resting its tonnage in a roundhouse in western Maryland. In 1989, an O gauge version of the Baldwin-built loco was offered to Lionel fans in all its 7-pound, 25-inch glory.

As if the Reading T-1 weren't enough, Lionel also announced its "Classics" line of big, steel Standard Gauge and O gauge designs from the 1920s and 1930s. The 44E box-cab electric in O gauge and a gray (not black) 384E Standard Gauge steamer, both with freight car consists, were the same trains Mike Wolf had been building under the MTH logo.

Lionel also announced a smaller Reading steamer, the 8004 4-6-2, and a set of extruded aluminum Amtrak passenger cars towed by an 8303 GG1 electric. Also chugging along on a power truck was a very nice little model of the ubiquitous Burro mobile crane, while in the back of their pre–Toy Fair catalog Lionel trumpeted their new "Railscope."

Video technology had progressed to the point where video cameras were small enough to squeeze into the most improbable places, from snaking down a person's esophagus for a peek into their stomach to security cameras the size of ballpoint pens. Lionel's techs had managed to wedge cameras into a selection of locomotives varying in size from HO to G scale. All that was visible was a square hole in the front of the engine for the camera's 22-millimeter lens. Images and instructions traveled through the rails to a black-and-white screen (requiring very clean track) for a train's-eye

In return, MTH would refrain from building any competitive products during that time. To sweeten the pot, Wolf was also offered a coveted Lionel authorized dealership. He convinced Samhongsa to go along with the deal and, in one swoop, Lionel had acquired a great design shop and offshore manufacturing to create wonderful new trains. Mike Wolf was guaranteed a steady income for five years; he hurried off to Samhongsa with a Lionel *Hiawatha* train set under his arm.

One of Wolf's first projects was to construct a model of the Reading 4-8-4 T-1 Northern locomotive. It seemed that Richard Kughn owned a full-size

Weaver's first brass locomotive, created by Samhongsa in 1990, was the Pennsylvania Railroad M1a 4-8-2 Mountain-type. Weaver ordered approximately 900 from Korea, setting aside about 50 for two-rail O scale operators, with the rest going to the three-rail "toy train" market. The latter sold out almost immediately. *Courtesy Weaver Models*

view of the layout. The concept was brilliant. The reality was something else. The system drained batteries by the bucketload, and the results were not always great on imperfect track. Railscope achieved its promise in the late 1990s when technology allowed color images, higher resolution, and even Dolby sound.

In 1991, an old chestnut was once again hauled out. The No. 672 Pennsylvania S-2 Turbine was an oft-reincarnated standby from Lionel's postwar renaissance. Every time sales started to slip, this veteran, based on a one-of-a-kind prototype, was spruced up and rolled out the engine shop door. This time, the old warhorse rumbled forth in spectacular style. A

full 30 inches long, the 6-8-6 engine and its huge scale-size tender (the prototype was large enough to carry 42 tons of coal and 19,500 gallons of water) featured their own sound effects—the hiss of the turbine blower—smoke, a glowing firebox, and constant-voltage lamps fore and aft. Watching this semiscale version of "The Big Swoosh" click out onto the mainline track at the head end of a long freight consist was a real Lionel moment.

In 1992, Wolf's design efforts produced a Western Maryland Shay locomotive that was quite amazing, considering its tinplate shell. Originally designed for logging and hauling on narrow O gauge track, the Shay type featured a steam engine that drove pistons mounted on the side of the locomotive, which, in turn, directly turned gears on the driving wheels. The concept was used for traction on steep grades and tight curves that snaked up the sides of heavily forested mountains. Wolf's engine epitomized the concept of Ephraim Shay as built by the Lima Locomotive Works. The irony was the Lionel logger couldn't run on the 27-inch radius of O27 track or the 31-inch-radius curves of O gauge. It required at least 54 inches of curve radius to get around a turn.

As all these new products were being offered, Lionel was taking steps to put the brakes on dealers who were dumping slow-moving trains, parts, and accessories at swap meets for well below list prices. Lionel's new dealer agreement stipulated that, to receive the official imprimatur as a "Value Added Dealer" (VAD), the recipient had to have a storefront, be listed in the local telephone directory, and

refrain from shoveling their slow sellers into the feeding frenzy at swap meets.

Around this time, the Wolf-Lionel partnership was heading for the rocks. According to Wolf, the in-house designers were revolting. They resented Wolf's influence on which products were built and the fact that his shop got most of the really neat designs. Wolf was also a squeaky wheel. He had complained about Lionel's huge production volume for high-profile trains and claims his warnings were ignored. However, in the 1992 catalog, Kughn announced Lionel was reducing production numbers, limiting each issue of hot locos and collectible rolling stock. As a result, collectors kept their eyes on any intelligence that indicated a pending new product release so they could pound down to their Lionel dealer and slap a reservation on the counter.

Another project Wolf claims to have championed was reviving the 1957 "Lady Lionel," a steamer with freight cars produced in pastel colors. The original offering laid a colossal egg—salesmen couldn't give the sets away to their own daughters, which made the set a rare collector's item.

K-Line, another Lionel competitor that was gaining ground rapidly decided its first entry into steam loco train sets would be what they called "The Little Girl's Train." It was virtually identical to Lionel's abortive 1957 experiment. K-Line's locomotive came from a 1984 mold of the No. 333 Marx Pacific steamer. To make the final model presentable, two years of upgrading features and fiddling with the mold passed between announcement and K-Line's delivery of the set. Although the set

The Dash 8-40B in Santa Fe yellow and blue freight colors modeled all-new four-wheel truck frames, dual motors, and a flashing roof light in 1990. *Courtesy Stan Roy Collection*

was produced specifically for the Toy Train Historical Foundation, it became part of K-Line's regular lineup.

Wolf's philosophy of countermarketing the competition drove his suggestion to bring back the Lionel version of the pink locomotive and its pastel consist. After initial resistance, Lionel eventually did produce the "Lady Lionel" again, and this time it sold well.

A 1990 rehash of the 1987 agreement between Lionel and MTH also trimmed back

Wolf's income from the original deal. In an attempt to recover some lost income, in 1992 MTH proposed production of a new Dash 8-40C locomotive in O gauge for Lionel. Lionel turned down the project and began cutting back the Classics line. Wolf's dream deal of constant income began sliding downhill.

In that same rather traumatic year, Wolf had severed his dealer relationship with long-time mentor, partner, and friend, Jerry Williams. Samhongsa, MTH, and Williams

When Marx tools and dies became available, K-Line engineers spent considerable time in a drafty storage facility looking for specific steam engine dies. They found the Marx 333 locomotive—Marx's only six-driver design—and worked it over into a Pacific-type to haul their replica of the pink Lionel "Girl's Train." This Pennsylvania Railroad version was announced in 1991, but arrived in 1993. *Courtesy MDK K-Line*

Reproductions had a falling out over a Williams cab-forward Southern Pacific loco that MTH sold for $1,300, but which Williams cut to $750.

Samhongsa found itself saddled with two locomotives built for Williams' premium Crown Line: the Pennsylvania T1 4-4-4-4 Duplex and the GG1 electric. MTH came to Samhongsa's aid by agreeing to finance the production.

To make up for this shortfall in income, Wolf needed some new revenue. Through dealers Frank and Jack Rash of Frank's Round-house, he met Bob Weaver of Quality Craft Models/Weaver Trains. He proposed to Weaver that, for a piece of the action, MTH would help Weaver offer Samhongsa-built brass trains Bob Weaver had been in the business since 1965, when he began turning out wood craftsman kits in many gauges for hobbyists. They had been gradually adding cars and diesel locomotives to their affordable line of plastic trains when the opportunity to jump into the premium brass market was presented.

Weaver Trains created their "Gold Line" of premium-quality locos and cars in 1990, starting with a splendid Pennsylvania Railroad M1A 4-8-2 Mountain class steamer. From there, they never looked back, and in December 1991 released the Pennsylvania Railroad T1 Duplex 4-4-4-4 as their seventh Gold Line model. They released their eighth model, the GG1, in February 1992.

The labyrinthine machinations of Wolf and his multimanufacturer relationships were simplified considerably in 1993 when he decided MTH would produce the Dash 8-40C diesel under their own logo. Wolf gave Samhongsa the go-ahead and created a brochure describing the loco in both 8- and 12-wheel configurations. In April 1993, at the big York (Pennsylvania) Train Meet, he set out a stack of the brochures in his booth. Kughn came down the aisle, picked up a brochure, read it, and invited Wolf to discuss matters further in Kughn's van. What occurred was a collision of two immovable objects. Kughn threatened to rescind Wolf's authorized dealership even though Wolf had $750,000 worth of unfilled orders for 1993 trains. A few days after the York meet, Wolf was bounced from Lionel and his dealership agreement torn up.

46

An early Alco FA diesel road engine built by K-Line from Kusan dies. This engine led the K-Line's motive power in 1987, as the company moved beyond track and rolling stock. *Courtesy MDK K-Line*

MTH and Samhongsa were left holding the bag for prepaid, unfilled Lionel orders and expanded manufacturing capacity with no big orders of their own to fill. The drop in income to MTH was more than a bit breathtaking. Unlike other Lionel competitors who had simply folded their tents and went away, Wolf hired the best lawyers he could find and filed an antitrust suit against Lionel. Attorneys representing Lionel countersued, claiming Wolf and MTH were trading on Lionel's name.

Of all the toy train lawsuits filed since the turn of the century, very few lingered long and were usually over patent infringements. With toy train competition heating up among a growing number of very good manufacturers in the 1990s, the MTH-Lionel lawsuit was serious business that would drag on for two years. For MTH, what began as a step-by-step climb up the ladder became a frustrating struggle and retrenchment. For Lionel, the housecleaning demand for market share now stretched into total war. On both flanks, smaller companies such as K-Line, Williams, and Weaver were luring away buyers with terrific, lower-cost trains and accessories. And all along, the computer boys in the backroom were figuring out how to stuff more and more features into this new generation of toy trains.

Another Lionel Large Scale shopped out in 1998 was this Milwaukee Road GP20. Lionel's 1998 comeback in Large Scale was fueled by the growth in garden railroading, whose practitioners were settling for European-looking trains. By the time Lionel made its move, American-type rolling stock was coming in from overseas. *Courtesy Mike Moore Toys and Trains/Bob Hanselman, Downers Grove Hobbies*

3

Competition and Computers Open the Market

Needless to say, the toy train marketplace was a real battleground by 1994. By virtue of its name and 93-year head start in the business, Lionel maintained a solid following of loyal fans. During Richard Kughn's watch, Lionel had lifted itself up by resurrecting classic locomotives, rolling stock, and accessories, and had also introduced exciting new models that transcended the "toy train" label. The new Northern T-1, the semiscale S-2 Turbine, contemporary diesels such as the Dash 8, and upgraded versions of long-gone Alco oil-burners gave the Lionel lineup considerable depth and excitement.

Though it's sometimes hard to believe, there is a finite number of locomotives and rolling stock to be modeled. Steam engines offer the widest field because the railroads ordered customized versions of each model shopped out by the likes of Lima and Baldwin. Some railroads, including Norfolk & Western at their Roanoke shops and the Pennsylvania Railroad at their famous Altoona Machine Shop and Juniata Works, even built their own locomotives for special purposes.

Every time a locomotive had an Elesco feed-water heater added above the smoke box or a booster motor attached to the trailing truck, there was another variation for the model-makers to offer.

Diesels, too, offer a variety of changes in addition to the upping of power from one generation to the next. From such "covered wagons" as Electro-Motive F units and Alco PAs and FAs, to "Geeps," SDs, U-Boats, TrainMasters, and "comfort cab" Dash 9s, there are always enough new variations to allow toy train makers to reintroduce old tooling with new features, or drop a new shell on an old frame and motor. When Lionel was virtually the only game in town, resuscitating "classics," and using tricks such as slicing a GP7's nose in half to produce a GP20, kept the brand afloat and moving forward. But in the 1980s, such reissues as the footsore 773 Hudson or the inevitable GG1 were challenged by new players who had access to the same superb tooling resources and computerized features.

Toy train hobbyists had become more sophisticated and the constant one-upmanship between the market leaders fueled demand for

Beating out Lionel's Pennsylvania T1 shrouded steam experiment by eight years, Williams created an exceptional brass version for its "Smithsonian Edition." They also offered the loco in bare brass at $595 with optional paint schemes available at $150. The loco only went forward, but a reverse unit could be added for $75, and if you wanted toots and hiss, you ponied up $175 for a True-Sounds plug-in. Only 650 were built. *Courtesy Williams Electric Trains*

50

In 1991, Weaver released a scale model of the GG1 in Tuscan Red and Brunswick Green with large lettering and a single gold stripe instead of the "cat whiskers" scheme. This model came out in 1993, incorporating a flywheel motor not offered the first time around. Following editions were released in various liveries, including Conrail, Amtrak, and Penn Central. *Courtesy Weaver Models*

even greater realism. This neck-and-neck bid for the buyers' bucks became even more intense as computers, lasers, and infrared systems moved out of the research and development shops and onto the rails. One of the first big technological breakthroughs was the arrival of digital sound.

Of course, toy trains crashed and rattled around the tracks back when they were still window displays in 1901. But only kids could provide the "whoo-whoo" until Lionel's wonderful, breathy whistle was introduced after World War II. Later, a dinging bell was added to the NW2 switcher and became so annoying that many dads yanked the wire. Lionel threatened to sue the pants off American Flyer if they didn't remove the patent-infringing whistle from their new K-5 loco, so A. C. Gilbert's design shop built whistling billboards that you triggered with a button as the train went past.

By 1995, K-Line had upgraded the original Kusan dies to produce this Alco ABA version of the MKT *Texas Special*, with considerable detail added. *Courtesy MDK K-Line*

Otherwise, American Flyer fans had to make do with an awful-sounding, onboard "Nathan Chime Whistle." There were also various geared "choo-choo" devices concealed in loco tenders and talking train stations, but the gears wore out and the "talking" voices became garbled after much use. With the 1990s, however, came computer chip technology, and all that changed.

Neil Young entered the picture in 1992. He recorded three music albums with Buffalo Springfield in the 1960s, and since 1969 has released more than 25 solo albums, worked with the supergroup Crosby, Stills, Nash & Young, and formed his own recording label, Vapor Records. More pertinent to our story, Young is a toy train hobbyist who takes great interest in its technology. His 4,000-square-foot Lionel layout, built in a barn on his Northern California ranch, had been keeping him and his son very busy at the time he met Kughn. They formed a partnership called "Liontech" to focus on computer chip breakthroughs.

Their first two innovations were an electronic reverse circuit board and RailSounds.

One of the problems with reproducing sound in locomotives was the medium upon which the sounds were reproduced. All analog mediums (audiotape and records) were too bulky. The advent of the EPROM (erasable programmable read-only memory) computer chip and a circuit board, combined with a small speaker, provided the answer. The sounds were recorded as small digital files and then "burned" into the chip. When toggled by an electrical current, the sounds were played back. The chips had previously been used in small HO locomotive tenders and diesels, so cramming them into a relatively huge O gauge machine presented no problem.

RailSounds was offered in two of Lionel's Large Scale locomotives. A 4-4-2 Atlantic with steam RailSounds chugged, blew its whistle, and hissed appropriately when it came to a stop. The diesel RailSounds allowed a GP20 to rumble at idle, while engine revs increased as

In 1995, another shrouded locomotive was added to Williams' Crown Line: the New York Central Streamlined *20th Century Limited* Hudson 4-6-4. Originally released in 1984, the 1995 version offered larger leading-truck wheels and more realistic rodwork cranking massive box-pox drivers. A deeper skirt almost covers the tender's wheels. *Courtesy Williams Electric Trains*

it started up—the engineer could even ding its bell with the activation button. RailSounds found its way into O gauge very quickly, providing a number of effects from which to choose, including DynaChuff, which timed the sounds of a chugging loco to the toy train's wheel speed, a labored chugging as the loco accelerated with a heavy load, diesel engine revolutions that increased from start-up, the dynamic braking as the loco headed down a grade, and steam blow-off. Eventually, Lionel also added CrewTalk, giving the illusion that the engineer and crew were in contact with the dispatcher and each other. The effects were so realistic that one almost expected to see a tiny engineer climb down from the cab and oil the drivers.

One very striking locomotive that offered RailSounds effects was the streamlined Chesapeake & Ohio Hudson No. 490 offered in the 1995 catalog. This yellow-and-silver diecast

In 1938, Otto Kuhler, designer of the Milwaukee Road's *Hiawathas*, answered the call for a streamlined steamer for the Lehigh Valley Railroad. The K-5 4-6-2 received Kuhler's shrouding, and joined the ranks of stunning steamers as the *John Wilkes*. This 1995 Weaver brass model with Proto-Sound captures that elegant—if short-lived—design. *Courtesy Weaver Models*

beauty packed all the sounds into its tender, and with the RailSounds activator built into Liontech's TrainMaster control, even more railroad noise could be made.

Not to be outdone by all this toot, hiss, and roar, Mike Wolf was very conscious of buyers' preference for locomotives that blew, honked, and grunted on cue. After being cut off from Lionel, he faced a major challenge to get his own business back into the black. His next planned locomotive was to be a huge scale model of an articulated Union Pacific Challenger

MDK K-Line:
The Little Engine That Did

Maury Klein began his career in toy trains at age four, while watching a battery-powered train circle a loop of track. He was puzzled and unsatisfied. At age six, he received a Lionel train set. He was no longer puzzled.

Maury's train collection began to grow, and by 1974, he was selling model trains through a small mail-order business while attending classes at the University of North Carolina. The more he sold, the more he realized that there was room for his own train company in the tinplate marketplace. Soon, on a plot of land near Chapel Hill, North Carolina, Maury constructed a building for his mail-order business. Shortly thereafter, in 1979, with the help of his father, Mark Klein, Maury and friends began building O27 and O gauge track under the name MDK K-Line. Maury Klein had found his calling.

By 1980, K-Line was producing both track and switches at costs well below Lionel's list. Klein's company remained well below Lionel's radar, however, as Fundimensions concentrated on filling the rolling stock and motive power pipeline. That situation changed rapidly, however, and by a circuitous route.

While K-Line was punching out tinplate track, one of the last great names in toy train history was filing for bankruptcy—again. In 1972, the Louis Marx toy train line had been sold to the Fisher-Price Toy Company, which was owned by another grain grinder: Quaker Oats. After a short honeymoon, Quaker Oats dumped the Marx line on another company that went belly-up and, in turn, dumped the Marx tools, dies, and oddments on the New York bankruptcy court.

Maury traveled to New York and picked up the Marxville dies for all the Marx buildings and accessories. In 1981, K-Line began turning out O gauge scale buildings as K-LineVille. By 1984, Klein dis-covered that some of the Marx locomotive dies were still available. In a scene out of *Indiana Jones and the Lost Tooling*, Klein and his plant manager, Brent Chambers, ventured into an unheated New York warehouse as snow wafted down on them from the holed ceiling. Amidst stacks of rusting, crumbling metal blocks, each containing the molds of locos and rolling stock, they rescued the 1947 Marx No. 333 Pacific steam engine and the No. 1829 Hudson, the only Marx locos with six drivers.

Their next acquisition was a collection of the peripatetic Kusan rolling stock dies. Kusan Model Trains (KMT) Corporation built plastic toy trains using dies made by Auburn Model Trains (American Toy Trains in an earlier life). In 1961, KMT bailed from toy train manufacturing and the dies were snapped up by Andrew Kriswalus for his Kris Model Trains Company. Kris sank in the early 1980s, however, and Jerry Williams bought many of the dies for Williams Reproductions. Williams used some of the molds for his own models before selling them to MDK K-Line in 1986.

K-Line's 1986 catalog featured track, buildings, and rolling stock at very affordable prices. Meanwhile, two KMT diesel locomotive molds, an Alco FA12 and an MP-15, were being reworked and updated by K-Line's research and development team.

Maury Klein's 1987 K-Line catalog opened to reveal train sets, track, and accessories that threatened to catapult the company into the industry's upper echelon, alongside Lionel, MTH, Williams, and Weaver. But while Klein offered quality products at low prices, he was still a step away from the premium-grade models of the competition. K-Line continued to inch forward until 1998, when they introduced a locomotive that stood the industry on its ear.

An unusual postwar streamlined steamer, the 1947 Baltimore & Ohio *Cincinnatian* was designed by Olive Dennis, one of the first female civil engineers in the industry. An elegant brass limited edition from Weaver in 1995 gives O gauge fans the same thrill that railfans experienced in the late 1940s. *Courtesy Weaver Models*

56

Marx Trains' charming 1999 take on the Henry Dreyfus–designed *20th Century Limited* was clever and very well done, considering the material limitations. Curiously, the matching oil-type tender was very similar in shape and size to the three passenger cars it would pull. *Courtesy Marx Trains*

4-6-6-4. He had two choices: create it in brass, which was easy enough, considering Samhongsa's capabilities, but would make it very expensive; or challenge Lionel and the competition by producing a diecast Challenger. After considerable debate, the diecast route was chosen, even though tooling would cost half a million dollars. As production moved ahead, MTH partnered with QSI, Inc., of Beaverton, Oregon, to develop a two-board sound system that would be built into MTH's top-of-the-line locomotives. They called their system Proto-Sound and hard-wired it into the

Challenger's tender. Later, they also offered the system as a retrofit option.

As with RailSounds, the MTH noise-maker eventually found its way into their Digital Command System Remote Control, incorporating 32 buttons to control everything from the engineer scratching his head (not really) to train station announcements (really). Owners could even record their own voice into the device.

Every competing builder quickly developed railroad sounds. K-Line unveiled their "Real Sounds" in 1999. Williams opted for

Atlas O is part of Atlas Engineering's 50-year tradition. Beginning in 1997, their offerings, including this 1998 model of a 1950 Electro-Motive switcher, soon won model railroad magazine awards. Atlas O is also one manufacturer that has licensed Lionel's TrainMaster Command and RailSounds to jump into the digital market. *Courtesy Atlas Model Railroad Company, Inc*

"True-Sounds" and offered it as an option. True-Sounds came with diesel motor sounds, bells, horns, and an adjustable volume, and required no special controller. Williams even supplied two-speaker stereo.

Weaver, who also wanted locomotives that wheezed and snorted, again turned to Wolf, who had cut a two-board audio system deal with QSI. With Wolf's help, Weaver ended up with a three-board QSI Sound System. In their 1992 catalog, their New York Central Dreyfus-shrouded Hudson featured "QSI Sound Compatible" as an add-on. Later,

they shifted their sound needs to OTT Machine, whose toots, plunks, and booms were very well received by Weaver fans.

Neil Young's Liontech also presented an open challenge to the industry in the form of technology that had previously been a much-sought holy grail: independent train control.

As early as 1946, Lionel had offered "Electronic Control" with a train set headed by a special version of the model 671 Pennsylvania S-2 steam turbine. Numbered the 671R, the loco towed a tender fitted with a radio receiving set. Each car in the set also had a radio receiver

In 1998, Lionel came back to Large Scale with a pair of diesels and rolling stock. Four DC can motors power this 7151 Pennsylvania GP9. It comes with a dynamic brake and lots of exterior detail, plus SignalSounds and directional lighting. *Courtesy Mike Moore Toys and Trains/Bob Hanselman, Downers Grove Hobbies*

Lionel built a fantasy locomotive in 1998—the *Phantom*—that was created, according to the accompanying storyline, in the 1920s, by a "secret society" whose "pure passion for train design" came up with this streamlined loco of unknown propulsion. The *Phantom's* market was also unknown. Lionel brought out the loco for $400 and a set of four futuristic passenger cars for another $400. *Courtesy Carail Museum, Detroit, Michigan*

and the whole operation was controlled by the ECU-1 push-button transmitter. Each button on the transmitter's panel operated a different function. In addition to controlling the loco's whistle, direction, starting, and stopping, the ECU-1 could activate the cars' electromagnetic couplers anywhere on the track and empty a coal car wherever needed. Ten different functions were sent through the tracks using 10 different radio frequencies. This was heady

60

The 4-6-0 wheel configuration has always been found under hardworking utility locomotives, and Bachmann's *Polar Express* is no exception. Imagine this train chugging past some snowdrifts. *Courtesy Bachmann Trains*

stuff in 1946, when the knuckle coupler itself was a huge breakthrough. Sadly, the idea was much better than its execution. Due to poor marketing, the radio's habit of wandering out of tune, the need for scrupulous track and wheel cleanliness, and a patent infringement lawsuit from a company who made radio-controlled dockside loading cranes, the "Electronic Control" sets were consigned to the scrap heap in 1950.

Liontech resurrected the dream of independent toy train control with a modular system called "TrainMaster."

With the 1994 version of TrainMaster, the engineer could operate multiple trains by creating segregated "blocks" of track, each wired to a PowerMaster unit. An operations area, such as a switchyard or a work siding, was isolated by using insulating pins as track joiners and was then powered with a Power-Master unit. Using a wireless TrainMaster hand-held controller, the engineer could work any of these isolated track sections

independently or all at once. As many as 10 locos could be operated at the same time using 10 PowerMasters. In effect, the Train-Master hand controller—called a Cab-1—was a minicomputer that commanded Power-Master blocks by means of programming commands punched in on the Cab-1 number pad. The brilliance of the concept also lay in its backward compatibility: any locomotive, from a postwar steamer to the latest Lionel heavy hauler, could be controlled with the 1994 TrainMaster system.

Besides operating the locomotives, the Cab-1 allowed the engineer to blow the whistle, ring the bell, add boost to a locomotive laboring up a grade, or apply braking on the downhill side. Two other buttons were added as TrainMaster evolved. Labeled "F" and "R" under the word "Coupler," they indicated that both the front and rear couplers could also one day be operated via TrainMaster, both a tantalizing tease and a throwback to the promise of the 1946 ECU-1.

With side pistons chugging, this Bachmann light Shay is very much at home in deep foliage, heading for a string of log cars at a camp near the compost heap. Garden railroading offers the perfect setting for geared locomotives that can climb steep grades. *Courtesy Bachmann Trains*

The year 1995 marked a new beginning in the manner in which toy trains could be operated, as well as an end to the era of Richard Kughn's command. The single-minded vision of Richard Kughn had brought Lionel from the brink of extinction to a dominant position in the toy train marketplace. In fact, his constant search for innovations and new directions had re-created that marketplace. In the early days of tinplate trains, when Joshua Lionel Cowen was at the helm, Lionel had frequently found itself chasing other manufacturers to match their new technology. Carlisle & Finch was the preeminent American toy train builder when Lionel was just a store window decoration. Dorfan pioneered diecasting; Ives created the best reversing unit; and Louis Marx controlled the low-end

volume market. During the late 1980s and early 1990s, however, everyone was chasing Lionel.

Liontech's breakthrough TrainMaster modular control system was upgraded in 1995 to a "command" system that sent operating instructions to each individual locomotive.

Electronic command and control systems were nothing new. Scale-model hobbyists running HO train layouts had competing computer-control systems to choose from. Circuit boards were crammed into the small diesel locos and steam engine tenders, allowing complete directional and speed control. Eventually, the board pin sockets in each locomotive were standardized by the National Model Railroaders Association (NMRA) so that any Digital Command Control (DCC) circuit board could be installed in any computer-ready loco. This concept had not reached the toy train market until Liontech introduced Lionel Command Control.

Lionel had proved to toy train operators that digital commands could be sent through the tracks for throttle and direction control. By adding a computer chip to the locomotive, and giving the chip a specific digital address, a number of functions could be controlled. In addition, by attaching a TrainMaster Command Base to the layout, the system could operate switches, accessories, and—the biggest kick of all—multiple trains on the same track.

But what if your Baby TrainMaster diesel rolled its freight consist onto a siding and you were needed elsewhere, say, to move dump cars along a work siding? New "ElectroCouplers" were triggered by those "front" and "rear" buttons on the TrainMaster controller, freeing your switcher to back out onto the mainline. Harking back to the original knuckle couplers of 1945, electromagnets were once again attached to each coupler, only the 1995 versions could be opened anywhere on the track. Only one detail of the 1946 ECU-1 promise remained to be fulfilled: ElectroCouplers were built only into locomotives, not rolling stock.

All of Lionel's high-end locomotives started rolling out of the shop equipped for TrainMaster Command Control, or with the ability to be upgraded to the system later on. The ElectroCouplers were also offered in kit form to upgrade earlier locos. As with the earlier version of the TrainMaster system, locos not equipped with chips—dating back to postwar antiques—are today able to run on the same tracks with the newest Lionel models. In this respect, the Lionel system is more sophisticated than HO Digital Command Control, which cannot mix computer-chip and non-chip locos because of the DCC engines' need for a constant 36 volts of track power.

Of course, this technological revolution also ensured an additional revenue stream, as engineers adapted their layouts to digital operation. Curiously, however, there was no stampede to buy TrainMaster equipment. The low-end, little-kid market was frozen out both by the lack of adaptable locos and by the complexity of the Cab-1's operation. Meanwhile, the older generation sniffed at the Cab-1 as a wary bear investigates a new garbage dump. The 250-watt, twin-throttle ZW Transformer introduced in 1948 was more to their liking. Some veteran collectors even removed the new Lionel digital reverse units and installed the old E-units in their place. Perhaps not surprisingly, the TrainMaster appealed to a core of operators accustomed to the new digital world, folks who had home computers, used cell phones, and kept track of their lives with PDAs (personal digital assistants). For them, the Cab-1 was a major step forward in toy train technology—as long as you didn't put anyone's eye out with its extended whip antenna.

Just as all this technology was revolutionizing toy train operation, and a whole new era of offshore production was creating incredibly detailed locos and rolling stock, Richard Kughn decided to call it a day. His stewardship at Lionel had given the whole industry a shot in the arm. He had hired good people, listened to customers, and energized toy train collectors and operators alike. He had also run roughshod over any small business or entrepreneur he targeted for making money off Lionel's name. By 1995, he'd had enough of the business and wanted to return to his collections, his Carail Museum, and his private life.

Neil Young asked Wellspring Associates LLC, an investment group that specialized in

Preceding pages: Weaver diecast diesels with good-looking details, including wire handrails, are still offered at reasonable prices. Examples of their craftsmanship are these RS11 and RSD12 Alco switchers. *Courtesy Weaver Models*

A pair of RS3 diesels demonstrates how technically sophisticated Weaver has become. The rear chassis supports an older chain-driven, single-motor loco. It is also silent. In the foreground is the latest in dual can motors, circuit boards, and lots of sound effects, all crammed into the same space. *Courtesy Weaver Models*

ailing corporate turnarounds, to make Kughn an offer. Unfortunately, there was still the unresolved lawsuit between Lionel and MTH. Lionel Trains, Inc., paid MTH an undisclosed settlement and the Lionel logo changed once again to Lionel LLC, managed by Wellspring. Gary Moreau, formerly of Oneida (the silverware people), came on board as the new president and CEO.

The Lionel catalog for 1996 wandered back in time by once again using illustrations instead of photography, titling the book "Lionel Corporation – 1996," and reissuing the *Commodore Vanderbilt*–shrouded Hudson and the 1950 773 Hudson, both with updated features. This bold journey through the past gave Lionel fans considerable pause.

Over in Northumberland, Pennsylvania, Weaver models were also undergoing significant changes. After the huge success of their first Samhongsa-built brass engine in 1990—the M1a 4-8-2 Mountain—they began issuing a steady stream of exceptional "Gold Edition" products, including the Lehigh Valley *John Wilkes* 4-6-2 Pacific for both three-rail and two-rail markets. The connection to the Korean manufacturer through Mike Wolf had elevated Weaver to the big boys' league. By 1993, however, following Wolf's departure from Lionel, Samhongsa once again devoted their entire manufacturing capabilities to MTH, dropping Weaver in the process.

By 1995, Weaver had introduced the Ultra locomotive line; their Baltimore & Ohio *Cincinnatian* and a version of the *John Wilkes* Pacific steamer were the first brass Ultra locos

released with sound. Also by this time, Joe Hayter, who had started at the bottom of the company, had worked his way up to the number-two spot, and in 1996 bought the company from Bob Weaver.

In 1995, K-Line's shops were just tooling up to release more new offerings in the next three years than they had produced in their first decade of operation. But because these were mostly O scale boxcars and a variety of rolling stock, K-Line remained below the radar of the major players. In 1997, however, K-Line produced an F7 A-B-A lash-up in which each unit was powered by two motors. Trumping that arrangement, they operated all three powered locomotives with a common electronic reversing unit through their trademarked PowerLink system. At the end of that three-year period, K-Line built a locomotive that turned the industry on its ear and cranked their reputation for fine engineering up another notch.

By the late 1990s, except for kiddy-level starter sets circling ovals of track, the term "toy trains" was becoming absurd. Fine-scale model motive power turned out by limited-edition brass engine makers for two-rail operation was being challenged by the scruffy tinplate crowd. While diecasting had matured into a fine art rather than a low-cost expedient, computer-generated electronics added sophisticated operation. As the millennium approached, the only way to tell the difference between tinplate and scale was by the depth of the flange and the number of the rails.

For sheer brawn and darkly handsome good looks, few locomotives surpass the Chicago & North Western E4 Hudson. This 1999 heavyweight models the big 84-inch drivers and high-speed capability of the prototype.
Courtesy MTH-RailKing

4

Offshore Production and the Computer Age

The first sentence of the 1998 Lionel Classic Trains catalog reads, "All locomotives, rolling stock and track in this catalog are made proudly at our manufacturing facilities in Chesterfield, Michigan, U.S.A." The catalog goes on to number a very few exceptions, but Lionel, at the time, was still the all-American manufacturer of three-rail toy trains. And in that effort they were virtually alone.

By 1998, all of Lionel's primary competition had headed across the blue Pacific to Korea and China, where skilled craftsmen turned out exquisite models at competitive prices. Having led the charge of fine-scale models built overseas, MTH continued to pressure Lionel by introducing the O gauge RailKing line in 1995.

The first locos were ambitious choices: New York Central and Santa Fe Mohawk steamers and the ubiquitous GG1. The RailKing line was intended to bite into Lionel's O gauge and O27 diecast markets. Designed to navigate tight turns, these lower-cost models were marketed to operators with smaller layouts and modest budgets. While the RailKing line was a significant step down from Mike Wolf's Premier and

Classic lines, Wolf still wanted it to feature a high level of value-added detail.

To keep costs down on the RailKing line, Wolf went hunting for a manufacturer in Asia. As luck would have it, the Chinese firm Waytechson was ending their relationship with Lionel. After giving Wolf a meeting, a tour, and a handshake, Waytechson left Lionel and shifted their production to MTH, creating a partnership that still exists today.

With Waytechson working on the Rail-King line, MTH needed something big and

The 1999 reissue of the O gauge *Commodore Vanderbilt* came fully equipped for $1,300. In addition to weathered and black versions, dealers were offered red and blue editions in production runs of 250 each. As special-design locos were issued in short runs, not all dealers could get one to sell, making buyers frantic to reserve certain models. This guaranteed-sellout strategy spans all manufacturers and wins no friends among dealers.
Courtesy Mike Moore Collection

attention-getting to challenge the limitations of tight-radius O gauge, a style established before World War I to accommodate the sharp turns necessary to cram maximum track into a minimum of carpet space. During a design meeting in Korea, Wolf saw what he wanted when he happened to glance at a designer's drawing board. The result was a 4-6-6-4 Challenger that could bend around those curves and not look ridiculous. After all, that was the reason for articulated locomotives in the first place: navigating tight turns while hauling heavy consists.

The model opened the door for even more innovative RailKing designs.

Although one-upmanship continued between the two toy train superpowers through 1996 and 1997, the big toy train breakthrough in 1998 came from neither Lionel nor MTH, but from K-Line: the Burlington Northern & Santa Fe GP38-2 road diesel.

K-Line designers had first spotted a GP38-2 working out of a yard near their offices. With cameras and notepads in hand, they took every opportunity to study the locomotive in

The SD70 MAC diesels of 1999, with six-wheel trucks and built to scale, were the result of new tooling and carried a full complement of Lionel electronics, including a can motor with a flywheel (allowing very slow speeds) and a lighted cab complete with engineer and fireman. *Courtesy Carail Museum, Detroit, Michigan*

"Hudson Madness" also descended over the industry in 1999 when everyone rolled out their own scale and semi-scale Hudsons. K-Line added their own semi-scale compressed version—a short-boiler look at this classic adorned with considerable detail. The toy train magazines loved it for its good looks and low price. *Courtesy MDK K-Line*

great detail. Back at their drawing boards, they produced scale renderings. In order to build what they had drawn and still keep the price below that of a brass model, the diesels were made of plastic and diecast and stamped-metal parts. The resulting detail was magnificent, from tiny lift rings on the long hood and operating fans beneath the exhaust ports, to the prototypical four-wheel trucks and the brass chain across the gap in the nose railings. The dual motors ran well and the couplers were operational. It was everything a budget-minded railroader could want at the head of a long freight—for only $333.

Meanwhile, three projects were under way at Lionel: one old, one new, and one for the future.

The old project was sustaining Lionel's Large Scale line with a pair of big diesels: a Pennsylvania Railroad GP9 and a Milwaukee Road GP20 in a garish orange and black livery. As Bachmann and LGB continued to introduce new American-style locomotives and rolling stock, the market for garden railroading steadily expanded. Although Lionel's models had, for the most part, been all but discontinued in 1996, the big locomotives and some freight cars were reintroduced in 1998. The following year, cartoonlike Large Scale Lionels were circling Christmas trees with decorated cars in tow. Clearly, Lionel still didn't have a handle on the market.

Lionel's Odyssey motor was another attempt at toy train immortality. Although Lionel had a tried-and-true motor in their Pullmor, they needed an improved design for their new, heavily detailed locomotives. Operators wanted long coal drags to sweep majestically through those 72-inch curves, and they

The Dash 9-44CW is a 390,000-pound diesel that generates 4,400 horsepower. The Lionel versions, introduced in 1999, have the same big-shouldered look and are fully tricked out with RailSounds, CrewTalk, TowerCom, ElectroCouplers, directional lighting, and a fan-driven smoke unit that generates fumes, which look just like scale-size, polluting diesel exhaust. *Courtesy Carail Museum, Detroit, Michigan*

wanted slow, prototypical speeds in the switchyard. New, imported slow-speed can motors had replaced the older skew-wound, open-frame designs that started locomotives at a neck-snapping 10 scale miles an hour and drove them up to 150 miles per hour with ease. Ideally, Lionel wanted to combine the slow-speed capability of the imported can motor with the open-frame design of the Pullmor, and build the hybrid in their Chesterfield,

Michigan, plant. The Odyssey was designed to work with the plethora of TrainMaster electronics found in most of the new locomotives, providing reliable pulling power, zero maintenance, and a sort of "cruise control" that would provide a constant running speed, regardless of steep grades. It also promised less power consumption, allowing more trains to run in any single power block. The dream never came true. And while the Odyssey

K-Line's most famous locomotive, their GP38b of 1998, showed the toy train industry that the company deserved a chair at the table. In BNSF livery, its detailing, paint, and fine-scale modeling were prime quality for its $300-plus price tag. *Courtesy MDK K-Line*

motor was replaced by can motors in 2001, the "Odyssey Speed Control" system remained.

The third project was an eccentric locomotive called the *Phantom*, a futuristic design that looked more like a test bed for stealth technology than a rail-bound engine. Appealing to an unknown audience, Lionel gave the *Phantom* a fictional background. It seems a secret group of professional railroad designers back in the 1920s, calling themselves the "Pratt's Hollow Design Society" (PHDS), pooled their know-how and came up with the *Phantom*. Made of some unknown composite material with an unknown power source, the resulting locomotive was the future of railroading.

The *Phantom* was gray and cost $400. In 1998, collectors could buy a four-pack of equally futuristic passenger cars for another $400, and in 2000, the *Phantom* was released in red. No red cars were built, however, and the Pratt's Hollow Dream Machine vanished again into the mists of time.

Also vanishing into the mists of time was Gary Moreau, the President of Lionel LLC. The numbers expected by Wellspring just weren't there during his watch, too many products had been delivered flawed, and several products that were promised had never been delivered. A Camelback 4-6-0 locomotive—a great-looking steamer with its cab straddling the

74

Snaking over a bit of curvy track is the darling of the 1999 launch year: the Union Pacific Big Boy 4-8-8-4 articulated locomotive. The 32-inch behemoth needs 72-inch-radius track. All-new tooling, together with a "centipede" oil-burning tender, gives the 4006 a massive look. The Big Boy also has RailSounds 4.0. The loco wasn't available until 2000 and then in limited quantities, causing long waiting lines at hobby shops. *Courtesy Carail Museum, Detroit, Michigan*

boiler—was promised in 1999, for example, but not delivered until 2000. As with the General Mills regime of the 1980s, Lionel was one revenue stream among many at Wellspring, and, as such, was expected to pull its weight. On July 26, 1999, Richard N. Maddox was appointed Lionel's president and chief operating officer.

Maddox was a train guy whose interest in the hobby can be traced back to age 15, when he worked as a clerk in a hobby store. His specialty was sales and marketing, which carried him to his appointment as vice president of sales and marketing at Associated Hobby Manufacturers, before he jumped to a similar position at Bachmann Industries. Before Maddox arrived there, Bachmann's HO line had a shaky reputation among modelers. All that changed in 1997 when Bachmann's Large Scale Shay won *Model Railroader* magazine's Product of the Year award. The following year, an HO 2-8-0 Consolidation, part of Bachmann's new Spectrum line, won the award in 1998 and turned the HO industry on it ear. Suddenly, everyone in the industry knew who Richard Maddox was. More great Spectrum products

followed, elevating the quality of Bachmann products from average to premier. And then Maddox brought his 40 years of industry experience to Lionel.

Immediately, he was faced with the bad raps of poor quality, slow delivery, and high prices. Many products had been rushed to market without thorough testing. MTH was producing numerous Lionel reproductions, and was selling them for less money. Overproduction of some Lionel rolling stock and locos had caused dumping, and cars that originally retailed for $400 could be purchased for $150 through mail-order houses. K-Line, Williams, Weaver, MTH, and Atlas O were competing with Lionel at all levels of the marketplace. The tarnished magic of the Lionel name and successful relationships he had established with manufacturers in the Far East were all that Maddox had.

In an interview in the August 4, 1999, issue of *Toy Train Revue*, when asked if he planned to eventually move all Lionel production to the Far East, Maddox responded, "Absolutely not. We certainly are going to produce more product in the Far East.... My guess is we're not changing anything here."

As Maddox settled into his office after pledging to keep Lionel, at least in part, the "Made in the USA" company, 1999 turned into a big year for toy train manufacturers, as they produced even better products and came to grips with the rigors of supply and demand. Having weathered the glut of 1997 and 1998 products that had buried dealers under mounds of expensive inventory, it was time to produce only what they could sell and to seek new distribution channels, including the Internet and television.

Lionel came out of the blocks with a Chesapeake & Ohio 2-6-6-6 Allegheny-type locomotive that weighed 17 1/2 pounds and stretched 32 inches. At the time, it was the largest and first articulated locomotive ever produced by Lionel. Its huge tender was connected to the locomotive by an infrared beam tether that transferred electronic signals for just about everything Lionel could stuff under the huge, diecast shells: TrainMaster Command directional lighting, and Articulated RailSounds 4.0 with CrewTalk, TowerCom, and DynaChuff. While this American toy train icon would shop out other articulated locomotives, the Allegheny succeeded in hauling Lionel's reputation to the top of the next hill.

As superdetailed locomotives and rolling stock—scale and semiscale in both brass and diecast—exploded into the market, the concept of "toy trains" was eclipsed by every manufacturer except one small shop in Wood Dale, Illinois.

Just as Joshua Lionel Cowen must have felt about Louis Marx when he looked over the fence and saw the former infantry sergeant looking back with a cheap tin locomotive in his hand, manufacturers today regard Marx Trains with a mixture of curiosity and respect. Marx Trains makes real toys today, just as Louis Marx did for nearly 65 years. In 1928, Louis created a company that built tin trains powered first by wind-up motors and later by electricity. His Joy Line trains were cute and clever,

Sorting Out the Big Trains

Though almost all toy train manufacturers today are selling into the "big gauge" garden railroad market, an interesting nonstandardization exists among these big engines.

Back in the dark ages of toy trains, when Lionel scooped everyone by copyrighting the name "Standard Gauge," Dorfan, Ives, American Flyer, and anybody else in the game had to use either "Wide Gauge" or "Number 1 Gauge" to advertise trains that ran on the same track. Today, the following variations exist:

Manufacturer	Scale	Designation
Bachmann	1:20.3	Large Scale
LGB	1:22.5	G Scale
Lionel	1:22.5	G Scale
Aristo-Craft	1:29	
USA Trains	1:29	
Märklin MAXI	1:32	1 Gauge
MTH-RailKing	1:32	One Gauge

All of these big trains run on the same 45-millimeter-wide track and all use compatible couplers (after adjusting for height with shims under the wheel bolsters). Their motors are generally AC/DC, use a circuit board to detect which current is available, and switch accordingly. However, track systems from different manufacturers are not interchangeable because of the methods used to connect the sections together. Go figure.

For movie buffs or railfans who want a touch of nineteenth-century steam on their pike, RailKing offered the 4-4-0 *Wanderer* diamond-stack star of the film *Wild, Wild West.* The 2000 steamer is diecast and thoroughly Proto-ized with digital electronics (as were the heroes, villains, and transportation depicted in Hollywood's most expensive Western to date). *Courtesy MTH-RailKing*

made of stamped steel (sometimes recycled soup cans), and lithographed in bright, kid-friendly colors. Marx made no pretense at realism in his early sets. Early M-10000 streamliners were stubby toys with turning keys in their sides. Some HO sets were sold with tin channel track that ran in a little circle. Later, however, Marx made full use of plastics to create good-looking trains that challenged Lionel's starter-set market. Though Marx owned the low end of the market, thanks to his distribution deals with fast-turnover dime

stores and department stores, Joshua couldn't resist challenging him with cheap Lionel sets. Lionel lost the price war every time.

Today, Marx Trains is owned by Jim and Debby Flynn, who completely embraced Louis Marx's philosophy by stamping out original locomotive and rolling stock designs using the same stamp-and-fold technology. In 1993, they sold out a run of locomotives and passenger cars in Canadian Pacific livery. Later, they produced a very credible Henry Dreyfus–shrouded locomotive and a matching set of passenger

Almost all of the toy train builders have had a crack at the EP5 electric. RailKing's 1999 O gauge version in ABS plastic celebrates the design that lived in the shadow of the GG1 for years. This tight-turning model can even live comfortably on O27 curves. *Courtesy MTH-RailKing*

cars. By the late 1990s, the Flynns had created a following that appreciated the whimsical and toylike quality of their trains.

At the far end of the spectrum from Marx Trains, clever toys grew a market that originated in Germany and was picked up enthusiastically by American manufacturers. Garden railroads were becoming quite the rage as the millennium loomed. Curiously, these big garden railroad trains have followed the same developmental path as the old Standard Gauge that Joshua Lionel Cowen stumbled upon back in the 1910s and 1920s.

The very first G scale (G, as in *gross*) trains in the world were imported to the United States by LGB (*Lehmann Gross Bahn*, or "Lehmann's Big Train") in 1968. The first engine to hit U.S. shores was the "Stainz," a little 0-4-0 that was definitely European in design, with its boxy looks, strange crosshead placement, and red trim. Early garden railroaders were content with the German trains, and created alpine layouts complete

with timber lodges and gingerbread stations. In 1984, however, LGB began building locos and rolling stock with an American flavor. The 2018D Mogul, a decorative brass, red, black, and white confection, was a take on the old diamond-stack wood burners that crossed the American prairies in the 1870s. There's no denying the craftsmanship and attention to detail on this locomotive. It proved to be the groundbreaking engine that sparked American interest in garden railroading. Soon, LGB was well entrenched in the American market.

In addition to continuing production of such popular European models as their RhB (Swiss *Rhatische Bahn*) electric locomotive in 1992 (its marker lights changed color, and its pantographs automatically raised, depending on its direction of travel), LGB rolled out new American types. The dual-motored Uintah No. 50 released in 1994 was an excellent articulated tank engine. This unique brute's prototype served the Gilsonite Mines in Utah along

For the sheer horror of a concept run amok, the Union Pacific No. 80 Coal Turbine's engine ate pulverized coal that created an exhaust temperature of over 780 degrees. A trailing tender carried enough nugget-sized coal for a 700-mile trip—that's 5,000 horsepower and 130,000 pounds of tractive effort. The 1999 MTH Premier Line's 54-inch model's A and B units were both dual motored. *Courtesy MTH-RailKing*

with its sister engine, No. 51. LGB also released two very recognizable diesels in the American marketplace: the F7a released in Santa Fe "war bonnet" colors in 1997, and an equally colorful New Haven F7 offered in 2001. LGB also rereleased their trademark Stainz 0-4-0 that year, this time with a stuffed bear from the world-famous Steiff Company as an engineer.

Noting LGB's burgeoning success with the garden railway crowd, Bachmann Industries joined the big-train fray in 1989, with an inauspicious battery-operated locomotive and consist that ran on plastic track. It was cheap, and its engine was operated with a hand-held remote control. Although the locomotive was an immediate hit, it was too unique to compete with the other big trains that were powered in a conven-

tional manner through the track. In 1990, to re-orient themselves with the market, Bachmann released the Big Hauler line of nineteenth-century 4-6-0 locomotives and freight and passenger cars, together with track and accessories, at a lower price point than competing products from LGB and Lionel. The *Polar Express* was typical of the line, with its smoke, sounds, and lighted passenger cars. In 1999, another Spectrum-line logger joined their award-winning two-truck Shay of the previous year. The light and very-well-designed tank engine ran on two can motors, giving it considerable hauling capacity as it negotiated steep grades.

In 2001, their centennial year, Bachmann introduced a collection of 2-6-0 Mogul-type locomotives that were joined by a series of 1876 4-4-0 American-type engines. In keeping

This Baldwin-built 2-6-6-2 articulated tank loco was one of two built for the Uintah Railway Company to haul Gilsonite from mountain mines. LGB's G scale model for 1999 was a great reproduction. After the railroad closed in 1939, Oregon's Sumpter Valley Railroad bought both prototypes, stripped off the saddle tanks and coalbunkers, and added coal tenders. The model offers both smoke and directional lights.
Courtesy LGB

with their nineteenth-century theme, these brassbound beauties were designed to haul Bachmann's antique passenger and boxcars.

Not wishing to be left out in the cold, MTH joined the big-train market in 2001, creating three classic locomotives in what it called "One Gauge." The modern behemoths, including the ubiquitous J3a New York Central Hudson or Dash 8 diesel, are loaded with digital goodies and available in any of five railroad color schemes. For a backyard that needs a heavy hauler to lug long drags up steep grades and over the compost heap, MTH offers a 4-6-6-4 Union Pacific Challenger.

As the 1990s came to a close, the big winners were modelers, hobbyists, collectors, and operators. Not since the early twentieth century had so many purchase options been spread over such a huge marketplace. In effect, enthusiasts at the end of the decade could model any era they preferred, from wood-burning diamond stacks to the latest bullet trains. They could also model in any gauge, from O27 to G, and pay anywhere from $300 to $1,000 for the same locomotive, depending on its scale details, method of construction (diecast or brass), and electronic innards.

Lionel was still the big dog, but only because of their name recognition among newcomers. Lionel quality was good, but their distribution system had become flawed: the Lionel Century Club allowed buyers to purchase products directly from the Lionel website, bypassing the dealers. Further, too many promised products had been delayed in the pipeline. Maddox and his team were just coming to grips with these problems as 1999 came to a close.

But Lionel wasn't alone with distribution and quality-control problems. MTH-RailKing was pumping out new models at a furious pace, but actually laying hands on them was another story. The good old days of dealer exclusivity were gone. Lionel and MTH could reside under the same store roof, along with Weaver, K-Line, Atlas O, and Williams. Unless buyers followed such magazines as Kalmbach's *Classic Toy Trains* and *O Scale Modeling*, their choices were bewildering.

For toy train buffs, 1999 through 2001 would prove exhilarating.

Weaver's Ultra Line of brass locomotives built offshore featured this Pennsylvania Railroad C-1 0-8-0 heavy-duty switcher in 2001. This 1/4-inch-scale model runs on a DC can motor, smokes, and can negotiate 31-inch O gauge curves. The engine also takes advantage of TrainMaster Command Control and RailSounds, benefiting from Weaver's licensing that technology from Lionel. *Courtesy Weaver Models*

Chapter

5

More Choices, Higher Quality, and Deeper Pockets

The year 1999 was pivotal for toy train manufacturers. Lionel was in danger of being eclipsed by MTH in sheer sales volume. Flank attacks by Williams, Weaver, K-Line, Atlas O, and Marx Trains threatened both low- and high-end models and chewed away chunks of market share. The targeted buying group was aging, and as more collectors and operators retired into fixed incomes, pockets became shallower and purchases became more selective.

Lionel came on strong, announcing its Union Pacific "Big Boy" 4-8-8-4. Following close on the heels of the articulated 2-6-6-6 Allegheny, the big hauler was but a flag bearer for the fleet of monster steamers to come. Though the Big Boy premiered at train shows across the country, the real deal didn't arrive until 2000. No matter: Lionel was waving its flag like crazy.

A triple lash-up of GP7 diesels was another 1999 offering. The three locomotives had Pullmor motors in the front and rear units, and each mounted a plastic shell on a metal frame beneath the Florida East Coast Railroad livery. The set was upgradeable to both Rail-Sounds and TrainMaster Command, holding the cost down to $800 for all three. Diesel lovers could also get a General Electric Dash 9-44CW in four different paint schemes and offered in either a "traditional" package (stripped of TrainMaster Command and RailSound electronics) or with the full complement of digital extras for another $100. The same option was available for a steam collection: two engine types mounted atop the same six-wheel-drive train and offered in eight road names. The operator could have a Hudson 4-6-4 or a Pacific 4-6-2. The green, black, and gold Southern Railway 4-6-2 was the best looking of the lot and didn't seem to be as compressed as the Hudsons.

More new Lionel tooling in 1999 took the form of big SD70 diesels in scale length. To top off the year, Lionel shuffled an old favorite back into the lineup. The *Commodore Vanderbilt* Hudson was re-rereleased, this time with a full load of electronic gadgetry and a choice of three shroud treatments: silver, black, and "weathered." As with other high-profile Lionel launches, the *Vanderbilt* was offered in very limited numbers—a dealer might be allotted only one locomotive.

A Denver & Rio Grande Western's 4-8-4 Northern-type locomotive turned out in 1/4-inch-scale handcrafted brass for 2000 is an impressive sight. Weaver's version needs a 72-inch curve of three-rail track. Baldwin built 14 of the locos for the D&RGW. *Courtesy Weaver Models*

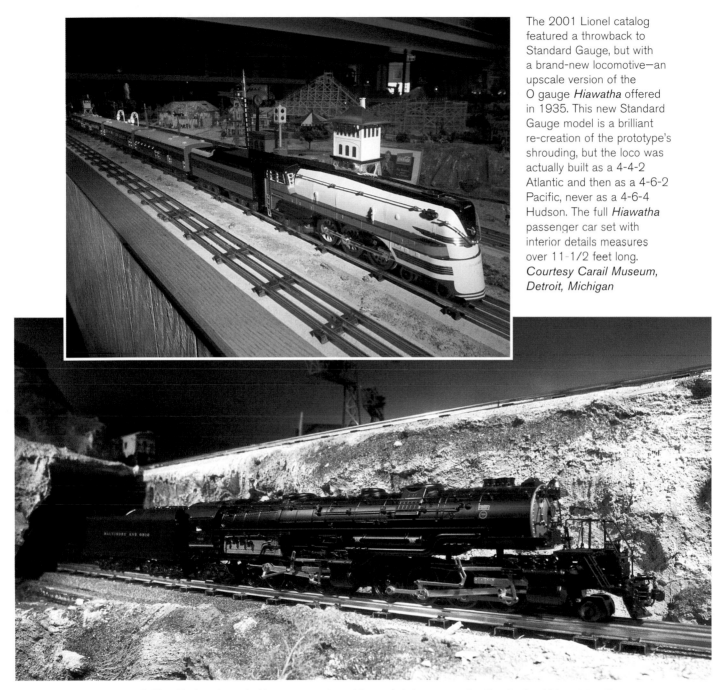

The 2001 Lionel catalog featured a throwback to Standard Gauge, but with a brand-new locomotive—an upscale version of the O gauge *Hiawatha* offered in 1935. This new Standard Gauge model is a brilliant re-creation of the prototype's shrouding, but the loco was actually built as a 4-4-2 Atlantic and then as a 4-6-2 Pacific, never as a 4-6-4 Hudson. The full *Hiawatha* passenger car set with interior details measures over 11-1/2 feet long. *Courtesy Carail Museum, Detroit, Michigan*

The Baltimore & Ohio Railroad needed horsepower to get long coal drags over the Cumberland Mountains. Between 1944 and 1945, 30 EM1 2-8-8-4 articulateds were built by Baldwin. Lionel's 2000 diecast scale model needed a 72-inch-radius curve and made use of an infrared "wireless tether" between the loco and tender. The ability to reproduce this level of detail in diecasting is a tribute to Chinese technicians. *Courtesy Carail Museum, Detroit, Michigan*

Not content with hot new diesels, in 2001 Lionel turned back to the 1930s with a set of three H-Class Consolidation 2-8-0 steamers. They represent old prototypes, but their innards are state of the art. Command Control and RailSounds moved along with a can motor. This No. 1111 represents the Pennsylvania Railroad H6sa steamer that survived until the 1940s. *Courtesy Carail Museum, Detroit, Michigan*

Over at MTH, Mike Wolf's Z-4000 Remote Commander hand-held wireless unit was unveiled as an alternative to Lionel's Train-Master. The Remote Commander controlled track power and could trigger Proto-Sound packages. Operators who preferred MTH equipment or a mixed bag of locomotives could now enjoy a wireless tether to their Z-4000 transformer. It was a step toward the MTH 2001 DCS (Digital Command System) that would talk to computer chips onboard DCS-equipped MTH locos, and finally achieve parity with the TrainMaster Command system.

MTH also brought out new locomotives—unique designs that didn't merely rehash old warhorses. The No. 80 Coal Turbine, based on an experiment by Union Pacific in 1962, was 54 inches long and required a 72-inch radius to haul very long freights. The diecast giant was powered by no fewer than four motors. Its QSI-built sound system featured numerous digital groans, honks, and hums.

To keep current, MTH also developed an Amtrak F59PH diesel—the successor to the F40PH Genesis—with sleek lines and an aerodynamic shovel nose designed to haul a five-car *Superliner* passenger set. Alongside the F59PH, the MTH Premier line P2 Boxcab Electric reflected a completely different era in full 1/4-inch scale (1/4 inch to the foot, like "true"

Resembling the silhouette of the Milwaukee Road *Hiawatha*, the Chicago & North Western *Yellow Jacket* was a pleasing nod to the tinsmith's art. Weaver's 2001 Ultra Line model is scale in size and—like Lionel's 1935 *Hiawatha*—requires a 54-inch-radius curve for three-rail operation. *Courtesy Weaver Models*

O scale). The P2 was a forerunner of the GG1, and MTH's new rendition sported dual motors and a full boat of digital features. It was the ultimate expression of the boxcab electric locomotive favored by toy train pioneers almost a century earlier.

The designers at MTH also managed to bring out yet another shrouded Hudson: the Chicago & North Western E4, a large, darkly menacing engine that looked as if it just emerged from the Bat Cave. Its prototype was the last C&NW steamer.

If the E4 was a new loco on the scene, MTH's version of the venerable EP5, often copied and squished for O gauge operation, was a welcome addition. This RailKing version, in both Great Northern and New Haven colors, featured correct six-wheel trucks instead of four-wheelers. It also negotiated O27 curves and came fully equipped with all the electronic goodies.

Keeping fantasy alive, MTH also gave us a movie locomotive, a model of the *Wild, Wild West* diamond-stack 4-4-0 wood burner designed for the movie of the same name. Like the prototype, the engine was equipped with state-of-the-art special features that Hollywood could appreciate. As if to remain in

MTH TinPlate Traditions' 2001 model of the Lionel 385 steam locomotive in Standard Gauge looks low-slung and brutal. It comes in its original gray with red-spoked wheels and copper trim over a core of computer-driven extras including Proto-Sounds 2.0. *Courtesy MTH-RailKing*

fantasyland, Mike Wolf's philosophy of countermarketing ran amok in 1999. While every other manufacturer brought out one shrouded locomotive, MTH—not content with just the E4—brought out two. Back in 1937, Reading created a one-of-a-kind streamlined Pacific type called the "Crusader." With the RailKing O gauge version in semiscale, toy train operators had two to choose from because Weaver also produced the loco in scale-length brass for 54-inch curves the same year.

With the theme of offshore production and limited editions set for the millennium, toy

train manufacturers pressed on into the new century with the most impressive collection of motive power and rolling stock ever produced for the hobby. But buyers had to be quick on their feet and fast with their wallets to snare a particular locomotive. If the corner hobby store didn't have the Lionel New York Central J3 Hudson an enthusiast desired, he or she could choose from Hudsons of at least equal quality and detail from MTH, K-Line, Weaver, and Williams.

Standard Gauge fans could purchase the latest *Hiawatha* passenger set from Lionel, or go

Made famous by the photographs of O. Winston Link, the Norfolk & Western Y6b 2-8-8-2 steam locomotive was shopped out by N&W's Roanoke shops from 1948 to 1950. It was a true "Mallet" design and the last of the type. The 2001 RailKing version takes advantage of the Y6b's articulation to swing through 31-inch-radius O gauge curves. *Courtesy MTH-RailKing*

to MTH Tinplate Traditions for an Ives 1764 Transition Electric or a truly fanciful, but beautiful, *articulated* 2-4-4-2 400AE—a gloriously goofy take on the old 400E. And if real *toy* trains were more desirable, Marx offered whimsical bread-loaf trolleys and Marlines freight sets, built of colorful lithographed tin in their Illinois plant. And, as of 2001, Marx Trains remained the only made-in-America toy train manufacturer,

Lionel LLC inevitably shut down their Chesterfield, Michigan, plant, clearing out all inventory and fixtures during a three-day auction in July 2000. With wonderful irony, Lionel's

last American-built locomotive was the Berkshire 2-8-4. Originally built in 1946 as the model 726, the "Berk" was a constant winner throughout the ever-changing Lionel regimes.

The other significant change at Lionel was the departure of Richard Maddox. On October 15, 2000, William Bracy took over as president and CEO. Ironically, Bracy worked for General Mills Fundimensions from 1970 to 1985, when that company was reviving Lionel's sagging fortunes.

In 2001, every manufacturer of modern toy trains bombarded the market with a dizzying variety of amazing locomotives, rolling stock,

Like a white ghost, the beautiful 3243R Ives Railway Lines Electric locomotive and matching passenger car set is a stunning addition to any Standard Gauge layout. The 2001 MTH TinPlate Traditions model re-creates for display only the 1920s Ives engine. *Courtesy MTH-RailKing*

accessories, and digital control—and in all gauges. In addition, K-Line and Weaver licensed the use of the TrainMaster Command system from Lionel, bearing witness to the intense competition that has driven a constant need to upgrade, form alliances, and create new products.

Today, giant articulated Big Boys, Challengers, EM1s, and the Norfolk & Western Y6s lumber down the main with long freight consists, while electrics, coal turbines, and diesels pass a variety of shrouded Pacifics and Hud-

sons rolling out of passenger yards. Electric train layouts have grown from circling Christmas trees to filling basements with swooping curves and steep grades. Backyard gardens resonate with wailing whistles, as diamond-stack steamers chug over real waterfalls and Dash 8 diesels drag grain hoppers past stubbly tulip beds and over tracks just recently cleared of snow.

Each manufacturer has developed a loyal following. Lionel owners remain steadfast to that iconic name. MTH followers revel in a

Bachmann released a series of Large Scale 2-6-0 Prairie-type locomotives in 2001. This "Centennial" series is a stunning collection, with rich details, good motors, the look of brass-banded boilers, and prototypical pluses including thrusting cowcatchers, kerosene headlamps, and holders for the marker flags. *Courtesy Bachmann Trains*

vast choice of locos and rolling stock. Weaver set a high standard in brass and then diecast motive power for three- and two-rail layouts, while K-Line raised the bar for more affordable products. Hobby store dealers who have constant-running window displays prefer Williams locos because of their ability to run and run and run without fault. Marx Trains appeals to the kid in everyone, who loves the charm of yesterday's toys.

Today's toy train enthusiasts revel in that smell of ozone mixed with wafting smoke,

the sounds of breathy whistles, blaring horns, and dinging bells. They smile upon hearing the click of steel wheels over three-rail track and the whine of dynamic brakes. The sight of long-gone steam engines brought back to miniature life, with churning valve gears rumbling past today's diesels in their gaudy paint schemes—this is the world of modern toy trains. It's a world with a legacy that dates back over 100 years and has given pleasure to millions who have controlled the throttles.

Bibliography

Chaverini Allen, Jacqueline. *Toy Train Story, A.*
    Columbia, MD: MTH Trains.

Drury, George H. *Guide to North American Steam Locomotives.*
    Waukesha, WI: Kalmbach Publishing Company.

Lavoie, Roland E. *Greenberg's Guide to Lionel Trains,
    1970–1991: Motive Power and Rolling Stock.*
    Sykesville, MD: Greenberg Publishing Company.

McComas, Tom and James Tuohy. *Lionel: A Collector's Guide
    and History, 1970–1980.*
    Radnor, PA: Chilton Book Company.

Ponzol, Don. *Century of Classic Toy Trains, A.*
    New York, NY: Barnes & Noble Publishing.

Souter, Gerry and Janet. *American Toy Train, The.*
    St. Paul, MN: MBI Publishing Company.

Souter, Gerry and Janet. *Lionel: America's Favorite Toy Trains.*
    St. Paul, MN: MBI Publishing Company.

Index

The American Toy Train
ISBN 0-7603-0620-6

Lionel: America's Favorite Toy Trains
ISBN 0-7603-0505-6

Classic Lionel Trains
ISBN 0-7603-1138-2

101 Projects for Your Model Railroad
ISBN 0-7603-1181-1

Vintage Slot Cars
ISBN 0-7603-0566-8

Racing and Collecting Slot Cars
ISBN 0-7603-1024-6

Diecast Cars of the 1960s
ISBN 0-7603-0719-9

Hot Wheels Cars
ISBN 0-7603-0839-X

Matchbox Cars
ISBN 0-7603-0964-7